WORLD-CLASS WAREHOUSING

EDWARD H. FRAZELLE, Ph.D.

LOGISTICS RESOURCES
INTERNATIONAL, INC.

ATLANTA, GA

Library of Congress Catalog Card Number: 95-81975

ISBN 0-9649893-0-1

Logistics Resources International, Inc.

3350 Cumberland Circle - Suite 1900

Atlanta, GA 30339

e-mail: 102430,2137 @ Compuserve.com

Agency: ZETA PERIODISMO

Graphic Designer: Javier A. Barrera

Cover Plan: Eng. Paul Le

Printed in Colombia by EDITOLASER

Impreso en Colombia por EDITOLASER

Dedication

This book is dedicated to my Lord Jesus Christ, my wife Pat, and my children Kelly and Andrew.

Acknowledgments

I have been blessed with world-class teachers, clients, and associates throughout my career in logistics. Clarence Smith, Jim Tompkins, John White, Jim Apple, and John Jarvis shared their logistics and life lessons with me. Ameritech, Amoco, Avon, the Baptist Sunday School Board, Bergen Brunswig, Ford, L.L. Bean, Lanier, Nashua, Owens & Minor, Spartan Stores, and Xerox allowed me the privilege to be their consultant and to describe their warehouse improvement projects in this book. Lee Marston and Bruce Strahan continue to encourage and challenge my teaching and research in logistics. Hugh Kinney and Dave Stallard make The Progress Group a learning and sharing organization. Karen Auguston had the patience to provide the style editing for this book. Freida Breazeal held up The Logistics Institute at Georgia Tech while this book was written. Maria Rey had the courage to accept me as her partner is this publishing venture. John White, Gunter Sharp, and Steve Hackman had the courage to advise me during my Ph. D. program. Kay Newman held up Logistics Resources International while this book was completed. Mark Nedza made the distribution of this book possible. Vic Carew and the Naval Supply Systems Command's Publication 529, the Warehouse Layout Planning Guide, provided many of the illustrations used in this book. My sincere thanks and deep appreciation go out to all of you.

TABLE OF CONTENTS

How to Read this Book

World-Class Warehousing was written with a variety of readers and reading styles in mind. Though I encourage you to read the book chapter-by-chapter, paragraph-by-paragraph, I have provided a number of reading aids to assist you including an extensive table of contents, numerous figures and sources, a variety of case examples, wide margins and margin notes, chapter summaries, and key references.

Table of Contents

Many of the lessons of *World-Class Warehousing* are contained in the ordered presentation of principles and systems. Hence, I insisted that the publisher include an extensive Table of Contents including all chapter headings, numbered sub-headings, and all other section titles. The Table of Contents can and should be used as a reading guide and as a checklist for your own warehouse improvement projects.

Figures and Sources

There are four types of figures in the book - system illustrations and photographs, concept illustrations, profiles, and analysis results. A majority of the system illustrations are taken from the Naval Supply System Commands *Warehouse Modernization and Layout Planning Guide*. Though published in 1985, it is still one of the best available references on warehousing systems. The other system illustrations and photographs were contributed by major system suppliers. A majority of the concept illustrations, profiles, and analysis results are taken directly from preliminary and final reports submitted in consulting assignments. In some cases the profiles and analyses were developed with the help of the Warehouse Toolbox™, a warehouse analysis and planning platform developed by the Logistics Technology Group in Nashville, Tennessee.

?

Case Examples

The book includes a variety of case examples taken directly from consulting and research engagements. In each case, an element of the case is used to illustrate a key principle or design guideline.

Margin Notes

The wide margins in the book are for two purposes. First, I encourage you to use the book as an inspiration for new operating concepts in your own warehousing operations; the wide margins can be used to record/illustrate those new concepts. Second, I have called out key principles into some of the margins. Those key principles can be read like a list of proverbs for warehousing. If you don't have time to read the book paragraph-by-paragraph, many of the book's lessons are contained in the margin notes and figures.

Chapter Summaries

Each chapter concludes with a summary which should be used as a checklist for applying the principles defined in the chapter.

References

The references and bibliography are not meant to be an exhaustive listing of warehousing papers and books. Instead, these are my personal favorites and in each case present their lessons quickly, clearly, and concisely.

INTRODUCTION: WHY HAVE A WAREHOUSE?

The best warehousing is no warehousing - so why should you read a book on warehousing?

1.1
SUPPLY CHAIN INEFFICIENCIES

Despite all of the initiatives in supply chain integration, efficient consumer response, quick response, and just-in-time delivery the supply chain connecting manufacturing with end consumers will never be so well coordinated that

The supply chain will never be so well coordinated that warehousing will be completely eliminated.

warehousing will be completely eliminated. However, as these initiatives take hold, the role and mission of warehouse operations are changing and will continue to change dramatically. This book holds up flexibility as the key to success in warehousing and describes how to increase the flexibility of warehouse operations through process design, system selection and justification, and layout configuration.

1.2
LOGISTICS ACCURACY

Supply chain integration initiatives to minimize pipeline inventory severely reduce the margin for error in supply chain logistics. Hence the accuracy and cycle time performance pressures in warehousing are immense. This book defines world-class accuracy and cycle time performance goals and defines the world-class processes that yield world-class accuracy and cycle time.

1.3
WAREHOUSE ROLES

A warehouse plays a valuable role in the supply chain by (see Figure 1.1):

- holding inventory used to balance and *buffer* the variation between production schedules and demand. For this purpose, the warehouse is usually located near the point of manufacture and may be characterized by the flow of full pallets in and full pallets out (assuming product size and volume warrant pallet-sized loads). A warehouse serving only this function may have demands ranging from monthly to quarterly replenishment of stock to the next level of distribution.

- accumulating and *consolidating* products from various points of manufacture within a single firm, or from several firms, for combined shipment to common customers. Such a warehouse may be located central to either the production locations or the customer base. Product movement may be typified by full pallets in and full cases out. The facility is typically responding to regular weekly or monthly orders.

- providing same-day delivery to key customers. Warehouses may be distributed in the field in order to shorten transportation distances to permit *rapid response* to customer demand. Frequently, single items are picked, and the same item may be shipped to the customer every day.

- serving as the facility where key product customization activities are executed including packaging, labeling, marking, and pricing.

This book describes the processes and systems required for the warehouse to satisfy each of these mission statements.

Warehouses may be distributed in the field in order to shorten transportation distances to permit rapid response to customer demand.

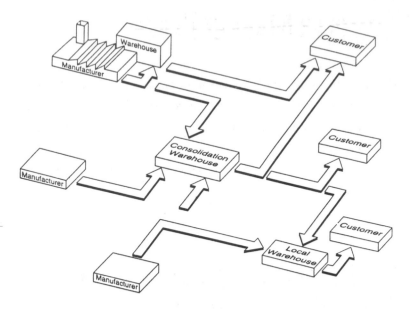

Figure 1.1 The role of the warehouse in the logistics chain [Apple].

1.4
WAREHOUSING COSTS

Warehousing is expensive - making up between 2% and 5% of the cost of sales of a corporation. With renewed corporate emphasis on return-on-assets, minimizing the cost of warehousing has become an important business issue. At the same time, continued emphasis on customer service places most warehouse managers between a rock and a hard place - looking for ways to trim costs and improve customer service at the same time. This book is written with this challenge in mind, and provides a variety of process improvement sugges-- tions aimed at improving warehouse resource utilization while maintaining and/or improving customer service.

1.5
COMPLEX MARKET PLACE

The warehousing marketplace is crowded with hundreds of suppliers of warehouse management systems, hundreds of third-party warehousers, and hundreds of warehousing consultants. This book was written to make you a better consumer in the marketplace, equipping you to separate the wheat from the tares.

Most warehouse managers are between a rock and a hard place - looking for ways to trim costs and improve customer service at the same time.

1.6
SEVEN PRINCIPLES OF WORLD-CLASS WAREHOUSING

World-Class Warehousing presents an organized set of principles that separate world-class warehouse operations from middle- and no-class warehouse operations. The principles were developed during a retrospective review of hundreds of warehousing projects including greenfield warehouse designs, warehouse layout designs, warehouse operations benchmarking, warehouse process improvement, and warehouse management systems design and implementation. These principles are the *common denominators* of the successful projects and successful warehouse operations. In order they are:

PROFILE

Create and maintain order profiles, item activity profiles, and planning profiles to identify root causes of process impediments and breakthrough opportunities for improvement.

order profiles
- item Activity profiles
- planning profiles

BENCHMARK

Benchmark warehouse performance, practices, and operating infrastructure against world-class standards to determine performance, practice, and infrastructure gaps; to quantify opportunities for improvement; and to estimate the affordable investment in new material and information handling systems.

SIMPLIFY

Simplify warehouse processes by eliminating as much work content as possible. Since most of the work in a warehouse is material and information handling, those two activities should be the focus of the process redesign initiatives.

[handwritten note in margin: Focus on material & information handling processes to simplify]

COMPUTERIZE

Incrementally justify and incrementally implement warehouse management systems, paperless warehousing systems, and decision support tools to maintain the warehouse activity profile; to track warehouse performance and resource utilization; and to enforce simplified warehouse processes.

MECHANIZE

Incrementally justify and incrementally implement mechanized material handling and storage systems to improve warehouse throughput and storage density, and to assist warehouse operators in difficult material handling activities.

LAYOUT

Layout the warehouse processes and material handling and storage systems to form a smooth flow of material and information between processes and to maximize floorspace and building cube utilization.

HUMANIZE CFOS

Humanize the warehouse operations by involving warehouse operators in redesigning warehouse processes; by developing team and individual performance goals; and by implementing ergonomic improvements in every manual activity in the warehouse.

[handwritten margin notes: Redesign Whse processes; Develop Team & Individual Performance goals; Improve Ergonomics In Every manual activity]

1.7
PRINCIPLES IN ACTION

Profiling (Chapter 2) and *Benchmarking* (Chapter 3) amount to doing your homework before an exam. In this case the exam is process redesign, material and information handling systems design, and systems implementation. The exam score is the new productivity, cycle time, accuracy, and storage density indicators for the warehouse. As is the case with academic exams, the better job you do in preparing for the exam, the better your exam score. Another way to think about this is that during the profiling and benchmarking process, no redesign has been set in stone and no money has been spent on new systems. It is during this stage of a re-engineering project that the most opportunity for improvement is available and the cost of design changes is the lowest. As a project moves from the preliminary concepting phase into detail design, implementation, debugging, and maintenance, the opportunity for improvement degrades and the cost of design

As a project moves from the preliminary concepting phase into detail design, implementation, debugging, and maintenance, the opportunity for improvement degrades and the cost of design changes increases exponentially!

Prep & Conceptual phase are Critical → Costs increase dramatically later

changes increases exponentially! As a result, the early preparatory and concepting phases of a project are the most important.

Simplification (Chapter 4) follows profiling and benchmarking because the project team needs the warehouse activity profile to creatively generate new, minimum work content processes and needs the benchmarking results to know the performance goals of the new processes and to know how much capital is available for new systems.

Computerizing (Chapter 5) follows simplification because the primary role of the computer is to enforce and monitor the new, simple processes. The warehouse management systems and paperless warehousing system requirements should flow naturally from the process definitions developed during simplification.

Mechanization (Chapter 6) follows computerizing because the simplification and computerizing process should minimize the amount of mechanization required.

Mechanization (Chapter 6) follows computerizing because the simplification and computerizing process should minimize the amount of mechanization required. Investments in mechanized systems are inherently less flexible than investments in computer software and hardware.

Layout (Chapter 7) follows mechanization because all of the warehouse entities required in the warehouse layout - process descriptions and material handling and storage systems - are not fully defined until the mechanization principle is applied.

Humanizing is the last of the seven steps not because the operators are the least important resource in the warehouse, in fact just the opposite is true, but because the full skill

26

set and cultural requirements for the workforce are not known until each of the first six principles has been applied. Since I am not an expert in human behavior or human resource organization, humanizing warehouse operations is not addressed in this book. (Please refer to [1] for more information on humanizing warehouse operations.) The only advice I can give in this area is very old advice - treat people the way you would like to be treated. Works every time!

Applied in this order, these principles can and have been used to create warehousing master plans, to re-engineer warehousing operations, to guide warehouse process improvement projects, and to develop requirements for warehouse management systems. I hope you will find them useful in similar projects.

Treat people the way you would like to be treated. Works every time!

If you are already familiar with the field of warehousing, please move onto the first step - profiling. If you are new to the field, the following review of warehousing basics may be helpful.

1.8
WAREHOUSING BASICS

The principles of this book are designed to solve the following problem - minimize total warehousing costs and satisfy the customer service policy. Total warehousing costs include the cost of labor, the cost of space, and the cost of material and information handling systems. These four resources comprise the warehouse operations infrastructure depicted in Figure 1.2. Since it is difficult to minimize something you cannot see, documenting and tracking these costs is an important remedial step on the way to world-class warehousing.

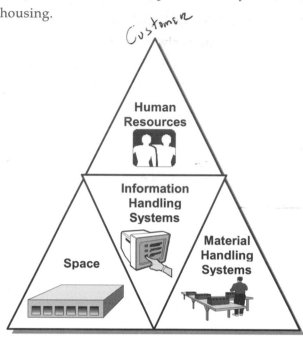

Figure 1.2 Warehouse operations infrastructure.

The customer service policy defines the services provided to different families of customers for inventory availability, response time, shipping accuracy, packaging, labeling, consolidation, returns, etc. Again, it is very difficult to satisfy something you cannot see. Another remedial step on the way to world-class warehousing is to document and tailor the customer service policy and track performance relative to customer service goals.

The key to achieving world-class status is to maximize the utilization and integration of warehousing resources while satisfying the customer service objectives and mission of the warehouse.

The key to achieving world-class status is to maximize the utilization and integration of warehousing resources while satisfying the customer service objectives and mission of the

28

warehouse. If you become consumed in minimizing cost, customer service will slide. If you become consumed with customer service, warehousing costs may increase too rapidly. Hence, identifying and implementing process improvements which simultaneously yield improved resource utilization and improved customer service are the keys to world-class warehousing and are the focus of this book.

The common denominator in those breakthrough process improvements is the elimination of work content.

The common denominator in those breakthrough process improvements is the elimination of work content. The majority of the work content in a warehouse is handling material and paperwork. To the extent you can eliminate that work content, you will be successful in your pursuit of world-class warehousing. The baseline of comparison for process breakthroughs is the traditional warehouse flow illustrated in Figure 1.3. The new processes and systems outlined in this book should be compared with this model to measure the extent of the process improvement.

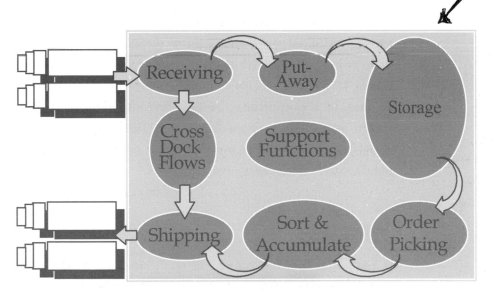

Figure 1.3 Traditional warehouse process flow.

1.9
WAREHOUSING FUNCTIONS

Traditional warehouse operations incorporate the following functions:

RECEIVING

is the collection of activities involved in (a) the orderly receipt of all materials coming into the warehouse, in (b) providing the assurance that the quantity and quality of such materials are as ordered, and in (c) disbursing materials to storage or to other organizational functions requiring them.

PREPACKAGING

is an optional activity and is performed in a warehouse when products are received in bulk from a supplier and subsequently packaged singly, in merchandisable quantities, or in combinations with other parts to form kits or assortments. An entire receipt of merchandise may be processed at once, or a portion may be held in bulk form to be processed later. This may be done when packaging greatly increases the storage-cube requirements or when a part is common to several kits or assortments.

PUT-AWAY

is the act of placing merchandise in storage. It includes moving material to and placing material in assigned put-away locations.

Storage

is the physical containment of merchandise while it is awaiting a demand. The form of storage depends on the size and quantity of the items in inventory and the handling characteristics of the product or its container.

Order Picking

is the process of removing items from storage to meet a specific demand. Order picking is the basic service a warehouse provides for its customers, and it is the function around which most warehouse designs are based.

Packaging and/or Pricing

may be done as an optional step after the picking process. As in the prepackaging function, individual items or assortments are boxed for more convenient use. Waiting until after picking to perform these functions has the advantage of providing more flexibility in the use of on-hand inventory. Individual items are available for use in any of the packaging configurations right up to the time of need. Pricing is current at the time of sale. Prepricing at manufacture or receipt into the warehouse inevitably leads to some repricing activity as price lists are changed while merchandise sits in inventory. Picking tickets and price stickers are sometimes combined into a single document.

Sortation

of batch picks into individual orders and accumulation of distributed picks into orders must be done when an order has more than one item and the accumulation is not done as the picks are made.

PACKING AND SHIPPING

may include:

- checking orders for completeness,
- packaging merchandise in an appropriate shipping container,
- preparing shipping documents, including packing lists, address labels and/or bills of lading,
- weighing shipments to determine shipping charges,
- accumulating orders by outbound carrier, and/or
- loading trucks (in many instances, this is a carrier's responsibility).

CROSS-DOCKING

is moving inbound material directly from the receiving dock to the shipping dock, essentially filling orders from receiving.

SUPPORT FUNCTIONS

include offices, truckers' lounges, restrooms, break areas, computer rooms, battery charging areas, etc.

WAREHOUSE ACTIVITY PROFILING

Suppose you were sick and went to the doctor for a diagnosis and prescription. When you arrived at the doctor's office, he already had a prescription waiting for you, without even talking to you, let alone looking at you, examining you, doing blood work, etc. In effect, he diagnosed you with his eyes closed and a random prescription generator. Needless to say, you would not be going back to that doctor for treatment.

Unfortunately, the prescriptions for many sick warehouses are written and implemented without either much examination or testing.

Unfortunately, the prescriptions for many sick warehouses are written and implemented without either much examination or testing. For lack of knowledge, lack of tools, and/or lack of time, many warehouse re-engineering and layout projects commence without any understanding of the root cause of the problems and without exploration of the real opportunities for improvement.

Warehouse activity profiling is the systematic analysis of item and order activity. The activity profiling process is designed to quickly identify the root cause of material and information flow problems, to pinpoint major opportunities for process improvements, and to provide an objective basis for project-team decision making. We will start with some of the major motivations and potential roadblocks to successful profiling. Then we will review a full set of example profiles and their interpretations. The examples will serve to teach the principles of profiling and as an outline for the full set of profiles required for re-engineering your warehouse or distribution center. We will finish with the data gathering, data compilation, data analysis, and data presentation process required in profiling.

2.1
PROFILING MOTIVATIONS AND MINEFIELDS

Done properly, profiling quickly reveals warehouse design and planning opportunities that might not naturally be uncovered. Profiling quickly eliminates options that really are not worth considering to begin with. Many warehouse re-engineering projects go awry because we work on a concept that never really had a chance in the first place. Profiling provides the right baseline to begin justifying new investments. Profiling gets key people involved. During the profiling process, it is natural to ask people from many affected groups to provide data, to verify and rationalize data, and to help interpret results. My partner Hugh Kinney says that, "People will only successfully implement what they design themselves." To the extent people have been involved, they feel they have helped with the design process. Finally, profiling permits and motivates objective decision making as opposed to biased decisions made with little or no analysis or justification. I worked with one client whose team leader we affectionately called Captain Carousels. No matter what the data said, no matter what the order and profiles looked like, no matter what the company could afford, we were going to have carousels in the new design. You can imagine how successful that project was!

You will see a lot of complex statistical distributions in our journey through warehouse activity profiling. Why go to all the trouble?

 Imagine we are trying to determine the average number of items on an order. Suppose we did the analysis based on a random sampling of 100 orders. In Figure 2.1, fifty orders are for one item, zero are for two items, and fifty are for three items. What is the average number of items per order? — It's two. How often does that happen? — It never happens! If we are not careful to plan and design based on distributions as opposed to averages, the entire planning and design process will be flawed. That is why it is so important to go to the extra step to derive these profile distributions.

My partner Hugh Kinney says that, "People will only successfully implement what they design themselves."

I worked with one client whose team leader we affectionately called Captain Carousels.

You can drown in a shallow lake - on average!

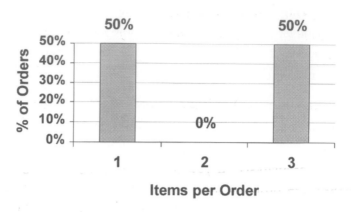

Figure 2.1 Example Items per Order Distribution.

When I write a new article or book, one of the first things I do to stimulate my own thinking is to read what other people have written about the particular topic. If I am preparing to teach a Sunday School class or a seminar, I do the same thing. I review what other people have prepared on the topic to stimulate my thinking and to avoid reinventing the wheel. {You know the difference between plagiarism and research - plagiarism is when you borrow from a single author, research is when you borrow from many.}

Wallowing in the data stimulates creative thinking!

Activity profiling works the same way. As you start to look at the profiles of customer orders, purchase orders, item activity, inventory levels, etc., the creative juices begin to flow for everyone on the project team! Everyone on the project team starts making good decisions and generating new ideas!

A picture is worth 1,000 words!

When you see a picture of a mother coddling her newborn baby, you experience a thousand simultaneous thoughts. We are aiming for the same effect in warehouse activity profiling as we paint a picture of what is going on inside the warehouse. In profiling, we are trying to capture the activity of the warehouse in pictorial form so we can present the information to management and so we can make quick consensus decisions as a team.

One warning before we begin to profile the warehouse (as an engineer and logistics nerd I fall into this trap a lot) - you can drown in your own profiles. Some people call this paralysis of analysis! If you are not careful, you can get so caught up in profiling that you forget to solve the problem. You have to be careful to draw the line and say, that is enough.

You can drown in your own profiles!

A full, yet minimum set of profiles required to plan and design your warehouse operations follows. This profile set is a synthesis of profiles built in a wide variety of warehouse project settings. They are presented to you as an example of the set of profiles you should have to effectively plan and manage your warehouse operations. The profile set stems directly from the seven key planning and design issues in warehousing (see Table 2.1).

2.2
CUSTOMER ORDER PROFILING

In general, material and information should flow through a warehouse to facilitate excellent customer service. What do customers really want from the warehouse? They want their orders filled. Then, the first thing we must understand to plan and design warehouse operations is the profile of customer orders.

Planning & Design Issue	Key Questions	Required Profile	Profile Components
1. Order Picking & Shipping Process Design	• Order Batch Size? • Pick Wave Planning? • Picking Tour Construction? • Shipping Mode Disposition?	Custumer Order Profile	• Order Mix Distributions • Lines per Order Distribution • Lines and Cube per Order Distribution
2. Receiving & Putaway Process Design	• Receiving Mode Disposition? • Putaway Batch Sizing? • Putaway Tour Construction?	Purchase Order Profile	• Order Mix Distributions • Lines per Receipt Distribution • Lines and Cube per Receipt Distribution
3. Slotting	• Zone Definition? • Storage Mode Selection and Sizing? • Pick Face Sizing? • Item Location Assignment?	Item Activity Profile	• Populary Profile • Cube - Movement / Volume Profile • Populary - Volume Profile • Order Completion Profile • Demand Correlation Profile • Demand Variability Profile
4. Material Transport Systems Engineering	• Material Handling Systems Selection & Sizing?	Calendar-Clock Profile	• Seasonality Profile • Daily Activity Profile
5. Warehouse Layout and Material Flow Design	• Overall Warehouse Flow Design-U, S, I, or L Flow? • Relative Functional Locations? • Building Configuration?	Activity Relationship Profile	• Activity Relationship Distribution
6. Warehouse Sizing	• Overall Warehouse Space Requirements?	Inventory Profile	• Item Family Inventory Distribution • Handling Unit Inventory Distribution
7. Level of Automation and Staffing	• Staffing Requirements? • Capital-Labor Substitution? • Level of Mechanization?	Automation Profile	• Economic Factors Distribution

Table 2.1 Warehouse Design Issues and Related Profiles.

A WAREHOUSE IN A WAREHOUSE

Some customers place such high demands on a warehouse, represent such a large portion of the activity in the warehouse, and have such high customer service requirements that it may make sense to establish a separate area within the warehouse for a particular customer or business unit - a warehouse within the warehouse. For example, a major apparel manufacturer does so much business with JC Penney that they have a JC Penney warehouse within their warehouse. A major distributor of packaging does so much business with May Company, that they have a May Company warehouse within their warehouse for May Company shopping bags. Third-party warehousing takes the warehouse within a warehouse notion to an extreme. In public warehouses, aisles within the warehouse are dedicated to specific customers. In contract warehouses the entire warehouse is devoted to the needs of a single customer.

As another example, many warehouses serve multiple business units under the same roof. This oftentimes is a major point of contention - the efficiency of shared resources versus business unit "control." (Via clever design and intelligent warehouse management systems you can have both.) For example, a large telecommunications company struggled through this tradeoff recently. It historically served four or five different business units from the same warehouse. Reserve inventory was commingled. Unique forward picking areas were established for each business unit. In this case, the argument for "business unit" control won out. The major reason was the lack of adequate warehouse management systems and organizational support to allow the managers of the warehouse to offer each business unit a tailored warehousing program. At the opposite end of the spectrum is another telecommunications company that has perfected tailored warehousing programs for diverse business units housed in the same distribution center. The company is so proficient at warehousing that they are considering entering the third-party warehousing business for their industry.

The company is so proficient at warehousing that they are considering entering the third-party warehousing business for their industry.

In another example (Figure 2.2), in a large publisher's distribution center, a central pool of reserve stock is used to support three distinct business units - retail, trade, and periodicals. Each business unit has allocated reserve inventory in the central warehouse and distinct forward picking zones to facilitate excellent customer service. The manager of each forward picking zone has a dotted line reporting relationship to the business unit to which his picking zone is reporting. The solid line reporting relationship is to the Director of Distribution. This is the best of both worlds - shared receiving resources, efficient handling of central inventory, dedicated forward picking lines, and shared shipping resources.

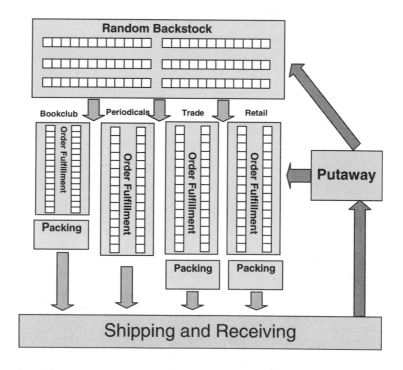

Figure 2.2 Example Warehouse within a Warehouse Concept [Warehouse Toolbox].

The warehouse within a warehouse design philosophy works because small warehouses, in general, have higher productivity and customer service performance than large warehouses (see Figure 3.4). The warehouse within a warehouse design philosophy allows us to divide and conquer the warehouse mission. Many of the customer order and item activity profiles are designed to identify opportunities to subdivide the entire warehouse operation into self-contained warehouse processing cells, virtual warehouses, or warehouses within the warehouse. This design approach is similar to that used in manufacturing where manufacturing activity profiles are designed to specify flexible manufacturing cells inside a large factory.

The warehouse within a warehouse design philosophy works because small warehouses, in general, have higher productivity and customer service performance than large warehouses (see Figure 3.4).

CUSTOMER ORDER PROFILE

The customer order profile includes the:
- order mix distributions,
- lines per order distribution,
- cube per order distribution, and
- lines and cube per order distribution.

The best way to explain each of these distributions and their interpretations is to review a series of examples.

Order Mix Distributions

There are a variety of order mix distributions that are helpful for plotting warehouse operating strategy. Three of the most helpful are the family mix distribution, the handling unit distribution, and the order increment distribution.

Family Mix Distribution

In many cases the overall operating strategy of the warehouse is dictated by the order mix - the extent to which orders require items from multiple families of items. If the orders are pure, i.e. tend to have just one of the families of items on them, then it is an early indicator that zoning the warehouse on that basis will create a virtual warehouse within the warehouse and will lead to good productivity and customer service.

The family mix distribution in Figure 2.3 comes from a wholesale distributor of fine papers, copy/laser paper, and envelopes. Category A is a family of merchandise called flat stock. Printers make high quality brochures from these flat stocks of fine papers. A carton of flat stock is about 30 inches long, 24 inches wide, and 9 inches deep. A carton weighs about 80 pounds. Category B is cut stock, basic eight-and-a-half-by-eleven copier and laser printer paper. A carton of cut stock is about 24 inches long, 10 inches wide, and 10 inches deep. A carton weighs about 20 pounds. Category C is envelopes and labels - extremely small and lightweight merchandise.

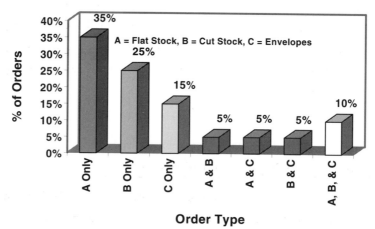

Figure 2.3 Example Family Mix Distribution.

In this example we are trying to figure out if it makes sense to zone the warehouse by those three item families - flat stock, cut stock, and envelopes. If the orders are mixed, i.e. flat stock, cut stock, and envelopes tend to appear together on customer orders, then in pallet building we would start with flat stock, put cut stock on top of that, and put envelopes on top of that. If that is the way we zone the warehouse, we may pay a big travel time penalty because we will have to travel across those zones or pass a pallet from one zone to the next.

If the orders are pure, i.e. they tend to be completable out of just one item family, then zoning the warehouse along these lines will establish efficient warehouse processing cells, especially since products tend to be received into the warehouse as flat stock, cut stock, and envelope shipments.

In Figure 2.3, 35% of the orders can be completed out of flat stock alone, 25% of the orders can be completed out of cut stock alone, and 15% out of envelopes alone. The good news is that (35% + 25% + 15%) 75% of the orders can be completed out of a single item family suggesting that zoning the warehouse by item family will yield good productivity, customer service, and storage density performance.

Handling Unit Mix Distributions

The full/partial pallet mix distribution and the full/broken case mix distribution are two revealing handling unit mix distributions.

Full/Partial Pallet Mix Distribution

With the full/partial pallet mix distribution we try to determine if we need separate areas for pallet picking and case picking. In some warehouses pallet and case picking are performed out of the same item location, aisle, and/or area of the warehouse. In general, it is a good idea to establish separate areas for pallet and case picking - replenishing a case picking line/area from a pallet reserve/picking area. This distribution simply helps reinforce the point and helps to identify warehouse within a warehouse opportunities.

In Figure 2.4, 50% of the orders are completable out of partial pallet quantities, i.e. just case picks; 30% of the orders are fillable from full pallet quantities, and the remaining 20% of the orders require both partial and full pallet quantities.

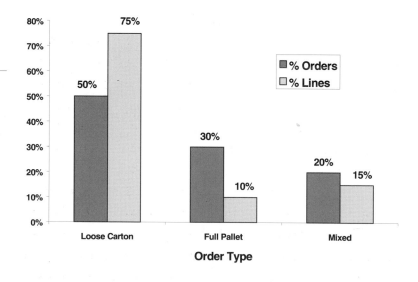

Figure 2.4 Example Full/Partial Pallet Mix Distribution.

WORLD-CLASS WAREHOUSING © EDWARD H. FRAZELLE PH.D.

Should we have a separate case picking and pallet picking area? If we did, would we pay a big penalty for mixed orders which require merging of the partial and full pallet portions of the order? — No, we really won't. That only happens 20% of the time. For 80% of the orders, zoning based on pallet/case picking creates a warehouse within the warehouse. When the orders come into the warehouse management system, it should classify them immediately as a pallet pick order, a carton pick order, or a mixed order. For mixed orders the warehouse management system should create a pallet portion, a case pick portion, and either pass the full pallet portion to the case pick area, or merge the case pick and pallet portions downstream from picking.

You now begin to see how we can quickly address the major planning and design decisions by having the right information available to us in the right format.

Full/Broken Case Mix Distribution

With this distribution (Figure 2.5) we try to determine if we should create separate areas for full and broken case picking. In some warehouses, full and broken case picking are performed out of the same item location, aisle, and/or area of the warehouse. In general, it is a good idea to establish separate areas for full and broken case picking - replenishing a broken case picking line/area from a case reserve/picking area. This distribution simply helps reinforce the point and helps to identify warehouse within a warehouse opportunities. As was the case with the pallet/case mix distribution in Figure 2.4, the distribution in Figure 2.5 indicates that only a small portion of the orders require both a full and

In general, it is a good idea to establish separate areas for full and broken case picking - replenishing a broken case picking line/area from a case reserve/ picking area.

broken case quantity. Hence, to create separate areas for full and broken case picking will yield two order completion zones with very little mixing between them.

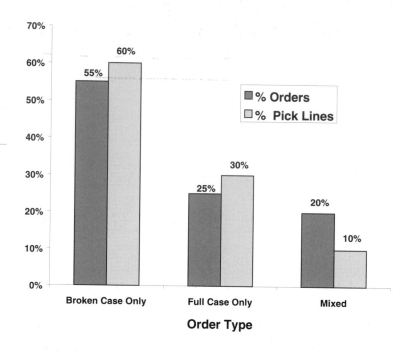

Order Increment Distributions

With the order increment distribution (Figure 2.6) we determine the portion of a unit load (in this case a pallet) requested on a customer order. For example, suppose there are 100 cartons on a pallet and a customer orders 50 cartons. In that case they ordered 50% of the pallet. If there are 80 cartons on a pallet and a customer orders 20, they ordered 20% of the pallet.

WORLD-CLASS WAREHOUSING © EDWARD H. FRAZELLE PH.D.

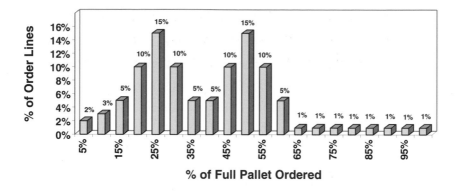

Figure 2.6 Example Pallet Order Increment Distribution.

What do you notice that is unusual about this distribution? (In almost all of these distributions the key insights are in the peaks and valleys.) Where are the peaks? The peaks are around a 25% and 50% of a pallet.

Suppose there are 100 cartons on a pallet and a customer places an order for 100 cartons. Would you rather pick a full pallet or 100 individual cartons? — You didn't have to buy this book to figure out that you would prefer to pick a whole pallet at a time. That is not only good practice for you, but it is good practice for your customer as well. The customer would rather receive a full pallet quantity that they can handle in one unit load as opposed to having to handle 100 loose cartons.

When a customer places an order for a quarter pallet, we have that unit load preconfigured.

Now, what operating decision should we make to take advantage of the distribution in Figure 2.6? Right, we should build some quarter- and half-pallet unit loads. Then, when a customer places an order for a quarter pallet, we have that unit load preconfigured. If a customer places an order for a half-pallet, we have that unit load preconfigured.

How can we build half and quarter pallet unit loads? In this particular case the manufacturing facility is attached to the warehouse. There is a palletizer that sits on the border and all we have to do is reset the palletizer to put a pallet in place about four times as often to build quarter pallets and twice as often to build half pallets! If the warehouse is not attached to manufacturing, the next best scenario is to have the supplier build the quarter and half pallet loads. And if not the supplier, then we can preconfigure the unit loads at receiving.

Can we encourage people to order in half, quarter, and/or layer quantity increments? Absolutely! In many cases by simply making the pallet/layer quantities accurate and visible to the customer and the order entry personnel via the logistics information system, we can encourage the practice of ordering in preconfigured unit loads. We can further encourage the practice by offering price discounts designed around efficient handling increments. In this case there was a representative from the sales organization on the cross-functional team who literally reset the price breaks on the quarter and half-pallet quantities the next day.

The two potential downsides of preconfiguring sub-pallet unit loads are (1) the complexities of mixing the practice with FIFO rotation requirements and (2) the loss of storage density. For FIFO rotation, the warehouse management system should be able to track date and lot rotation within FIFO windows. I believe in many industries FIFO requirements are named falsely as an impediment to world-class warehousing practices. As an example, I recently worked with a candy company

In many cases by simply making the pallet/layer quantities accurate and visible to the customer and the order entry personnel via the logistics information system, we can encourage the practice of ordering in preconfigured unit loads.

that continued to hold out FIFO as a barrier to productivity improvements. *I can remember a design meeting on Valentines Day when the company was receiving product for the next Halloween season. Indeed, there can be some large time windows within the FIFO requirements.*

There will be some loss in storage density since a pallet worth of cartons may now have 2 or 4 pallets supporting it for some unit loads. For half pallet quantities, we should be able to stack 2 halves in a full opening. For quarter pallets, we may need a row of openings that are 15% taller than the opening for singles. As a result, the loss in storage density should be less than 5% for the entire warehouse. And, the profile should tell us the potential productivity yield associated with the new practice. If the yield is such that the loss in storage density is offset, the practice should be implemented. If not, the practice should not be implemented. The ability to make that decision objectively is the reason to have the profile!

With the case order increment distribution (Figure 2.7) we determine the portion of a full carton that is requested on customer orders. For example, if there are 100 pieces in a carton and a customer orders 50, the customer ordered half the carton. What do you notice that is unusual about this distribution? In this case (Figure 2.7), customers tend to order around half a carton and a quantity close to a full carton. As a result, we would like to set price breaks at a half carton (and create an inner pack for a half-carton) and at a full carton to encourage customers who are almost ordering that quantity now to order in full carton increments.

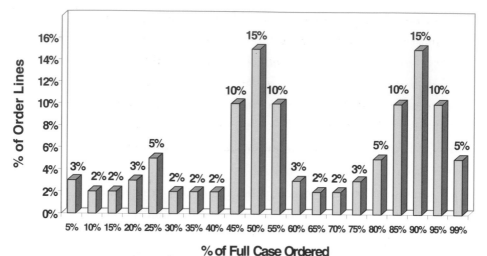

Figure 2.7 Example Case Order Increment Distribution.

✗ _The general principle is to prepackage in increments that people are likely to order in and to encourage customers to order in intelligent handling increments_. A higher level principle is that the supplier should do as much as possible to help prepare the product for picking and shipping. After we negotiate to have the supplier do as much for us as possible, then we should do as much as possible at the receiving dock to get product ready for shipping and packing, because it is at that moment that we have the largest time window available for picking/shipping preparation. As soon as the order drops for that product, the handling and preparation of the product should be at a minimum to meet the ever shrinking time window for product delivery.

Lines per Order Distribution

The lines per order distribution in Figure 2.8 indicates that 50% of the orders in the warehouse are for one line item,

WORLD-CLASS WAREHOUSING © EDWARD H. FRAZELLE PH.D.

15% for two, 15% for three to five, 10% for six to nine, and 10% for ten or more. Where is the peak? It is around single line orders. This is not uncommon, especially in the mail order industry or in cases where individual consumers or technicians are placing orders on the warehouse. We now need to consider the operating strategies which take advantage of this order profile.

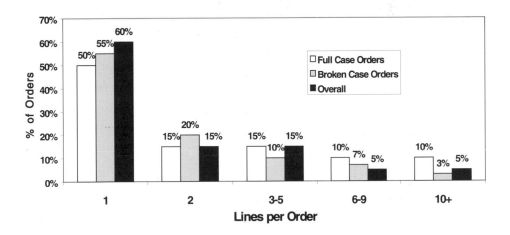

Figure 2.8 Example Lines per Order Distribution.

First, "singles" may be backorders. Backorders are an excellent opportunity for cross-docking. Second, "singles" may be small, emergency orders. Those orders can be batched together for picking on single-line picking tours, and by printing single-line orders in location sequence we create efficient picking tours! In addition, the order batches naturally divide the warehouse into zones defined by the length of the picking tour. Third, single-line orders may also represent an opportunity to create a dynamic forward pick line.

We should do as much as possible at the receiving dock to get product ready for shipping and packing, because it is at that moment that we have the largest time window available for picking/shipping preparation.

In this operating scenario, an automated look-ahead into the day's or shift's orders may yield a number of SKUs for which there is at least a full-carton's worth of single line orders. Those SKUs can be batch picked and setup along fast pick-pack lines.

Another common lines per order distribution is the mirror image of Figure 2.8. The peak is around ten plus lines per order. This is common in retail/grocery/dealer distribution where the customer is a retail store/grocery store/dealership. In that case, there is typically enough work to do within an order so that the order itself represents an efficient workset. Or, the order may be so large that it may be split across multiple order fillers for zone-wave picking.

Lines and Cube per Order Distribution

The lines and cube per order distribution (Figure 2.9) brings together in one profile the critical information needed to define order picking strategy. It is a joint distribution that classifies all orders into *lines per* and *cube per* families. It illustrates the typical daily picking activity. In this example (Figure 2.9) there are 176 orders with one line item and that occupy less than a cubic foot of space. Those orders are probably candidates for a single operator to batch together for picking into compartmentalized picking carts, totes, or shipping containers. There is one order with more than 10 line items that occupies more than 20 cubic feet, about a third of a pallet. That order is a candidate for a single operator to pick to a pallet.

WORLD-CLASS WAREHOUSING © EDWARD H. FRAZELLE PH.D.

Lines per Order	Cubic Feet per Order						Totals	% Orders	Total Lines	% Lines
	0-1	1-2	2-5	5-10	10-20	20+				
1	176	15	16	7	3	3	220	49%	220	17%
2-5	100	24	27	15	10	2	178	40%	623	47%
6-9	8	6	6	6	4	3	33	7%	248	19%
10+	2	1	1	6	4	1	15	3%	225	17%
Totals	286	46	50	34	21	9	446	100%	1,316	100%
% Orders	64%	10%	11%	8%	5%	2%	100%			
Total Cube	143	69	175	255	315	270	1,227			

Figure 2.9 Example Lines and Cube per Order Distribution.

PURCHASE ORDER PROFILING

The purchase order profile includes the same distributions (order mix distributions, lines per order distribution, and lines per order distribution) as the customer order profile. The only difference is that the activity is inbound instead of outbound. The purchase order profile is used to make the same batching and processing strategy decisions as was the customer order profile except the batching and processing strategies are for receipts and putaways as opposed to order picks. Keep in mind that your purchase order is your supplier's customer order. The structure is the same, a list of line item numbers, descriptions, and quantities. The only difference is that the purchase order is inbound to your warehouse and the customer order is outbound from your warehouse.

The purchase order profile is used to make the same batching and processing strategy decisions as was the customer order profile except the batching and processing strategies are for receipts and putaways as opposed to order picks.

This chapter focuses on the customer order profile because a single receipt/putaway may represent many bin trips for order picking. All of the distributions that make up the purchase order profile will not be presented because the purchase order profile is the customer order profile in reverse. That is not to discourage you from creating it for your warehouse. In fact, it is a critical and revealing part of the warehouse activity profile.

Item Activity Profiling

The item activity profile is used primarily to slot the warehouse, to decide for each item (1) what storage mode the item should be assigned to, (2) how much space the item should be allocated in the storage mode, and (3) where in the storage mode the item should be located. The item activity profile includes the following activity distributions:

- popularity distribution,
- cube-movement/volume distribution,
- popularity-volume distribution,
- order completion distribution,
- demand correlation distribution, and
- demand variability distribution.

Just like a minority of the people in the world have a majority of the wealth, a minority of the items in a warehouse generate a majority of the picking activity.

Again, the best way to describe each distribution and its interpretation is by example.

ITEM POPULARITY DISTRIBUTION

Just like a minority of the people in the world have a majority of the wealth, a minority of the items in a warehouse generate a majority of the picking activity. The popularity distribution (sometimes called an ABC curve or a Pareto Distribution) indicates the x% of picks associated with y% of the SKU's (ranked by descending popularity). Figure 2.10 is a classic popularity distribution indicating that the 10% most popular items represent 70% of the picking activity, the 50% most popular items represent 90% of the picking activity, and so on. Dramatic breakpoints in the distribution may suggest item popularity families. For example, the top 5% of the items (Family A) may make up 50% of the picking activity, the next 15% of the items (Family B) may take us to 80% of the picking activity, and the remaining 80% of the items (Family C) cover the remaining picking activity. These families may in turn suggest three alternative storage modes - Family A in an automated, highly productive storage mode, Family B in a semi-automated, moderately productive picking mode; and Family C in a manual picking mode that offers high storage density. The family breakpoints may also suggest the location of the items within a storage mode. A items located in the *golden zone* (close to a travel aisle and/or at or near waist level), B items in the *silver zone*, and C items in the remaining spaces.

The overriding principle is to assign tne most popular items to the most accessible warehouse locations. Unfortunately, many warehouse operators use the wrong measure of popularity. Some use dollars sales, some use usage, and some use the number of requests for the item. In the end, all of these are wrong!

The family breakpoints may also suggest the location of the items within a storage mode. A items located in the golden zone (close to a travel aisle and/or at or near waist level), B items in the silver zone, and C items in the remaining spaces.

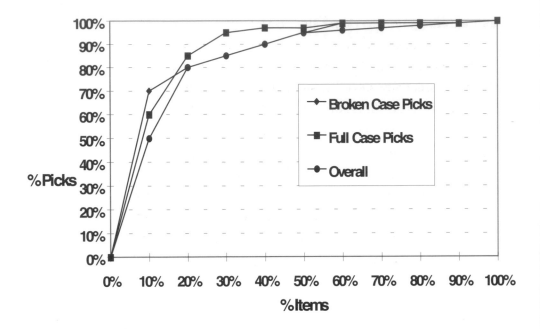

Figure 2.10 Example Item Popularity Distribution.

The number of requests for an item is the true measure of popularity, however, it is not enough information to assign items to storage modes or even to locate items within storage modes. The proper assignment of items to storage modes and allocation of space within the assigned storage mode is based on the popularity distribution *and* the cube-movement distribution. From the joint popularity-cube- movement distribution we can make appropriate slotting assignments.

Some use dollar sales, some use usage, and some use the number of requests for the item. In the end, all of these are wrong!

CUBE-MOVEMENT DISTRIBUTION

The most revealing distribution for determining storage mode and space allocation decisions is the cube-movement (or volume) distribution. The cube-movement distribution

WORLD-CLASS WAREHOUSING © EDWARD H. FRAZELLE PH.D.

indicates the portion of items that fall into pre-specified cube-movement ranges. If the pre-specified ranges correspond to storage mode alternatives, then the cube-movement distribution will essentially solve the storage mode assignment problem. For example, in Figure 2.11 15% of the items ship less than 0.1 cubic feet per month. Those items may be good candidates for storage drawers or bin shelving. At the other end of the distribution we find 12% of the items that move more than 1,000 cubic feet (nearly 20 pallets) per month. Those items may be candidates for block stacking, double-deep rack, push-back rack, and/or pallet flow lanes. *The principle is to assign items to storage modes based on their cube-movement.*

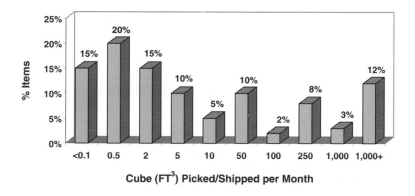

Figure 2.11 Example Cube-Movement Distribution.

POPULARITY-CUBE-MOVEMENT DISTRIBUTION

Done properly, slotting takes into account both the item popularity distribution and the cube-movement distribution.These distributions can be combined into a joint distribution. An example popularity-cube-movement distribution for broken case picking is presented in Figure 2.12.

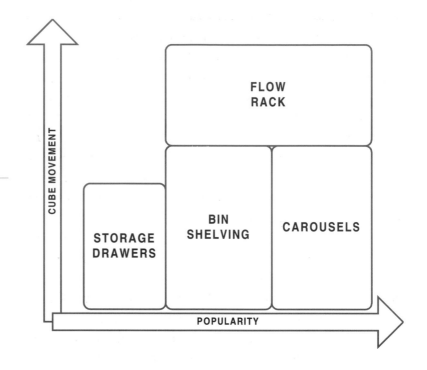

Figure 2.12 Example Popularity-Cube-Movement Distribution
for Broken Case Picking.

In the example, those items exceeding a certain cube-movement threshold are assigned to carton flow rack. Items with high cube-movement turnover often need to be restocked frequently, and need a larger storage location as compared to items with medium and low cube-movement. Hence they need to be assigned to a storage mode that facilitates restocking and condenses large storage locations along the pick line-carton flow rack. Items with low cube movement and high popularity generate many picks per unit of space and do not occupy much space along the pick line. They need to be in a highly productive picking mode. In this case light directed carousels are recommended because the picking productivity is high, and we can afford the carousels for items that do not need large storage housings on the pick line. (Carousels do not lend themselves to restocking and are expensive per cubic foot of space.) Items with low popularity and low cube-movement cannot be justifiably housed in an expensive storage mode. Hence, they are candidates for bin shelving and modular storage drawers. Once the storage mode assignments have been made, the preference regions for each storage mode become their popularity-cube movement distributions. Those items in the bottom right-hand portion of the distribution generate the most picking activity per unit of space they occupy in the storage mode. Hence, they should be assigned to positions in the golden zone. Those items in the upper right hand and lower left hand generate a moderate number of picks per unit of space they occupy in the storage mode. Hence they should be assigned to positions in the silver zone. Finally, those items in the upper left hand quadrant of the distribution generate the fewest picks per unit of space they occupy and they should be assigned positions in the bronze (least accessible) zone.

This example is not meant to make an end-all recommendation for slotting broken case picking systems. That depends on many other factors including the wage rate, the cost of space, the cost of capital, the planning horizon, etc. Instead, this example is presented to illustrate how the popularity-cube-movement distribution is used in the slotting process. Once in place, the distribution provides most of the insights required for slotting the entire warehouse, the subject of section 4.5.

Item-Order Completion Distribution

The item-order completion distribution (Figure 2.13) identifies small groups of items that can fill large groups of orders. Those small groups of items can often be assigned to small *order completion zones* in which the productivity, processing rate, and processing quality are 2-5 times better than that found in the general warehouse.

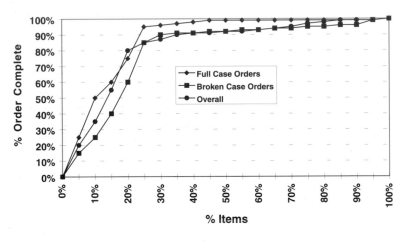

Figure 2.13 Example Item-Order Completion Distribution.

Those small groups of items can often be assigned to small order completion zones in which the productivity, processing rate, and processing quality are 2-5 times better than that found in the general warehouse.

The item-order completion distribution is constructed by ranking the items from most to least popular. Beginning with the most popular item, then the two most popular items, then the three most popular items, etc. the items are put against the order set to determine what portion of the orders a given subset of the items can complete. In this example 10% of the items can complete 50% of the orders. Suppose I walk into your warehouse and identify 10% of the items that can completely fill 50% of the orders. What would you do with those 10%? I hope you would create a warehouse within the warehouse or order completion zone for those 10%.

The design principle is similar to that used in agile manufacturing, where we look for small groups of parts that have similar machine routings. Those machines and those parts make up a small group technology cell wherein the manufacturing efficiency, quality, and cycle time are dramatically improved over those found in the factory as a whole.

I recently worked with a large media (compact discs, cassettes, videos, etc.) distributor and helped to identify 5% of its 4,000 SKUs which could complete 35% of the orders. We assigned those 5% to carton flow rack pods (3 flow rack bays per pod, 1 operator per pod) at the front of the distribution center. Operators could pick-pack orders from the flow rack at nearly 6 times the overall rate of the distribution center. The distribution center has won its industry's productivity award for the last two years.

DEMAND CORRELATION DISTRIBUTION

Just like a minority of the items in a warehouse make up a majority of the picking activity, certain items in the warehouse tend to be requested together. The demand correlation distribution (Figure 2.14) indicates the affinity of demand between individual items and between families of items. In the example, pairs of items are ranked based on their frequency of appearing together on orders. We are looking for general patterns. In this case we are examining data from a mail order apparel company. The first three digits represent the style of the item (i.e. crew neck sweater, V-neck sweater, turtle neck shirt, pleated pants, etc.), the middle digit represents the size of the item (1=small, 2=medium, 3=large, 4=extra large), and the last digit represents the color (1=white, 2=black, 3=red, 4=blue, 5=green, etc.).

Item Number	Item Number	Pair Frequency
189-2-4	189-2-1	58
493-2-1	493-2-8	45
007-3-3	007-3-2	36
119-2-1	119-2-7	30
999-1-8	999-1-6	22
207-4-2	207-4-4	15
662-1-9	662-1-1	12
339-7-4	879-2-8	9
112-3-8	112-3-4	6

Figure 2.14 Example Demand Correlation Distribution (Style-Size-Color).

What do you think people tend to order together from this mail order apparel catalog operator? (I thought it would be shirts and pants that looked good together in the catalog.) What does the distribution in Figure 2.14 suggest? In this case customers tend to order items of the same style and size together. The explanation is that customers tend to get comfortable with a certain style and tend to order in multiple colors to add variety to their wardrobe. Of course they order the same size unless they will return one for fitting. This was a surprise to me.

WORLD-CLASS WAREHOUSING © EDWARD H. FRAZELLE PH.D.

More importantly, it was a surprise to the marketing people. That is the most important reason to go through the profiling process - to surface the truth! (Unfortunately our intuition about logistics issues is often off-base. The myriad of SKUs, order patterns, suppliers, and interdependent decisions make it difficult to form reliable intuition about logistics operations.)

How do we take advantage of this demand-correlation information in slotting the warehouse? We are looking for the lowest common denominator of correlation, the factor that will create the largest family of items. In this case it is the size of the item. So, we zone the warehouse by item size first, creating a zone for the smalls, mediums, larges, and extra larges of all styles. Within each size area, we store items of the same style together, mixing colors within a style. This zoning strategy allows us to create picking tours based on size and style. As a result, order pickers can pick many items on short-distance picking tours. At the same time, we manage congestion by spreading out the sizes. Golden zoning is used to store the most popular color for each style at or near waist level.

Unfortunately our intuition about logistics issues is often off-base. The myriad of SKUs, order patterns, suppliers, and interdependent decisions make it difficult to form reliable intuition about logistics operations.

DEMAND VARIABILITY DISTRIBUTION

The demand-variability distribution (Figure 2.15) indicates the standard deviation of daily demand for each item. Unfortunately, an item's daily demand is not predictable. During a recent project we were trying to size the pick faces along a case picking line such that each pick face held a day's worth of stock. The motivator was to make sure that we did not need to restock a location during the day. The current design had the pick faces sized for an average day's demand, and the client could not figure out why they had to restock so many locations during the course of the day. I hope you see why. If the pick face is sized for the average day, unless the same quantity is picked every single day, there will be many days when the pick face is oversized and many days when the pick face is undersized, thus requiring a replenishment.

The real objective was to make sure that there was no need to restock during a picking shift (2 pick shifts per day and 1 restocking shift per day). Hence, the pick face must be sized to accommodate the average day's demand plus enough to cover 1 standard deviation of demand for a 5% chance of restocking and 2 standard deviations of demand for a 1% chance of restocking. Once the pick faces were resized to accommodate this variability of demand, the restocking during the pick shift was virtually eliminated.

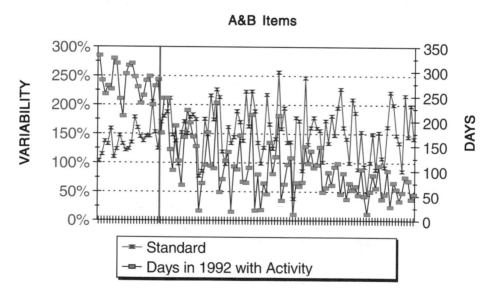

Figure 2.15 **Example Demand Variability Distribution.**

2.4

INVENTORY PROFILE

The inventory profile includes the item-family inventory distribution used to reveal opportunities for improved inventory management practices and the handling unit inventory profile used in storage systems planning.

ITEM-FAMILY INVENTORY DISTRIBUTION

The item-family inventory distribution indicates the amount of inventory on-hand by item popularity family. In this example from the textiles industry (Figure 2.16) there are 40 million yards of product on-hand for A items (80% of sales & 5% of items), 20 million yards for B items (15% of sales & 15% of items), and 19 million yards for C items (5% of sales & 80% of items). A items turn 30 times per year, B items 10 times per year, and C items 4 times per year. What's wrong with this picture?

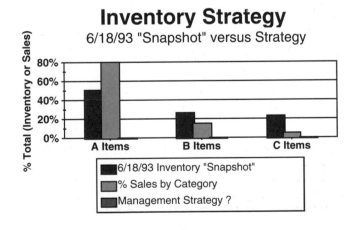

Figure 2.16 Example Item-Family Inventory Distribution.

I receive a lot of phone calls that begin with a client complaining about the lack of space in his or her warehouse. *More often than not the problem is not too little space, but too much inventory.* This profile helps us identify the source of the inventory problem. As is true in the example, most companies have too little A inventory (backorders and customers screaming for those products) and too much C inventory (obsolete stock that nobody wants and nobody has the courage to discard). By drawing the picture we can at least illustrate the magnitude of the problem to management and present a list of "problem" items for their review.

In some cases the C items should be removed from inventory. The problem may be the lack of a formal item inventory review program. In this case the profile helps identify the candidates for removal.

In many cases, however, you are forced to house the C items. One example is in the service parts business, where you may be required to support a certain model number in the field for up to 5, 10, even 20 years. Another example is in retailing when some key C items protect the sales of the A and B items. On a recent project in the grocery industry, the chairman of the company was presented with a recommendation to eliminate the C items from inventory. Let's pause and consider the consequences. How many items do you buy on your weekly trip to the grocery store to restock the kitchen cabinets? Say it's 50 items. In that case there is at least a 70% chance that one of those 50 items is a C item. Why did you go to that grocery store? In the case of this grocery chain, it was probably because they stocked that C item.

Even though you may not be able to eliminate the C inventory in some cases, you can at least be efficient in the way you store and pick the items. To conserve space, you may want to store the C inventory in dense, high-rise racking or on the 2nd or 3rd level of a mezzanine. To get good productivity at the same time you may want to batch pick the C-item pickline and locate the batch in a dedicated location along the forward pick line or introduce the batch into an automated sortation system.

To conserve space, you may want to store the C inventory in dense, high-rise racking or on the 2nd or 3rd level of a mezzanine.

HANDLING UNIT INVENTORY DISTRIBUTION

The item-family inventory distribution is not very useful for storage systems design because the information is not presented in material handling terms (i.e. pallets, cases, eaches, etc.). This is a common problem with most corporate data used in planning warehouse operations - the data is expressed in terms of dollars, pounds, pieces, days of supply, turns, etc.. Though useful for business planning purposes, the data is not very helpful for planning and managing warehouse operations. That is another motivation for the profiling exercise - to give the managers and designers of the warehouse operations a presentation of the warehouse activity in their terminology.

In this example (Figure 2.17), we convert the item-family inventory distribution into a distribution describing on-hand inventory in terms of pallets of merchandise on-hand. As a result, we can recommend the appropriate mix of pallet storage modes. For example, the 10,000 SKUs with less than a pallet of inventory on-hand should probably be stored in shelving or decked racking. The 1,200 SKUs that have 1 or 2 pallets on-hand should probably be stored in single-deep pallet rack. The 500 SKUs that have 3-5 pallets on-hand should probably be stored in double-deep and/or push-back rack. The remaining SKUs, those with more than 10 pallets on-hand, should probably be stored on the floor in deep block stacking lanes, in drive in/thru rack, and/or in pallet flow lanes.

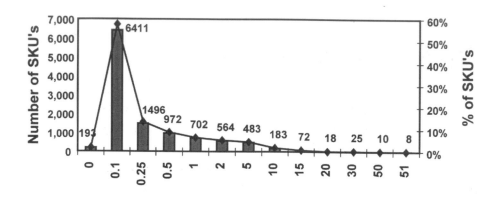

Figure 2.17 Example Handling Unit Inventory Distribution
[The Progress Group].

2.5

CALENDAR-CLOCK PROFILE

The calendar-clock profile includes a *seasonality distribution* and a *daily activity distribution*. The distributions are designed to reveal peaks and valleys in warehouse activity so that material handling systems can be properly sized and so that proper staff scheduling programs can be designed.

SEASONALITY DISTRIBUTION

The seasonality distribution (Figure 2.18) indicates the peaks and valleys in inventory levels as well as receiving, shipping and returns activity. Since storage systems need to be sized to accommodate near-peak inventory levels, and material handling systems need to be sized to accommodate near-peak activity levels, it is critical to identify peak inventory and activity levels. The example is typical of retail distribution with receipts peaking in August/September, inventory peaking in September/October, shipping peaking in October/November, and returns peaking in January. A distribution like this also indicates an opportunity for workforce shifting by moving the extra staff required for receiving in August/September to shipping in October/November to returns handling in January. (In the extreme, an employee could receive an item, put it away for storage, pick it for shipping, and return it into the warehouse.) With the seasonality distribution in hand, a popular rule of thumb for planning purposes is to design systems to accommodate the average day of the peak week.

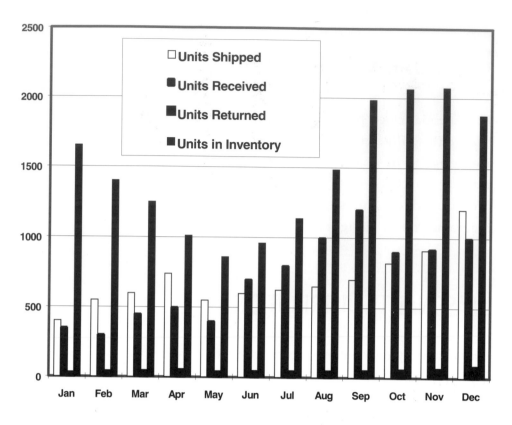

Figure 2.18 Example Seasonality Distribution.

DAILY ACTIVITY DISTRIBUTION

The daily activity distribution (Figure 2.19) indicates hourly peaks and valleys in receiving, storage, picking, and shipping activity. Material handling systems should be designed for peak activity periods and offsetting peaks represent opportunities for shift staggering and interdepartment workforce shifting.

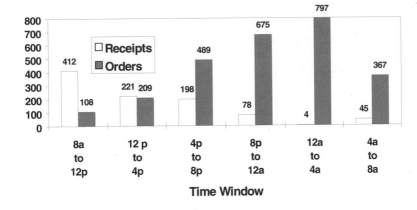

Figure 2.19 Example Daily Activity Distribution.

ACTIVITY RELATIONSHIP PROFILE

The activity relationship profile and distribution (Figure 2.20) reveals the inter-functional and inter-process relationships in the warehouse. It is used to suggest the location of processes and functions relative to one another in a block layout. An example activity relationship profile follows. In the example we simply record under each inter-process relationship the importance of locating the processes adjacent to one another. For example, it is critical that reserve storage be adjacent to receiving staging for efficient putaway (of course receiving staging would be eliminated in a world-class warehouse).

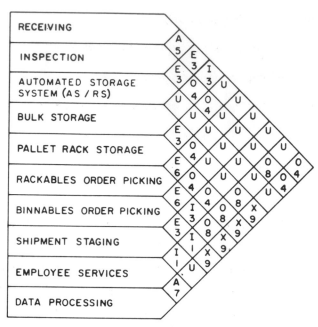

RECEIVING

INSPECTION

AUTOMATED STORAGE SYSTEM (AS / RS)

BULK STORAGE

PALLET RACK STORAGE

RACKABLES ORDER PICKING

BINNABLES ORDER PICKING

SHIPMENT STAGING

EMPLOYEE SERVICES

DATA PROCESSING

REASONS FOR IMPORTANCE

1. Supervision
2. Safety
3. Material flow
4. Work flow
5 Material control
6. Equipment proximity
7. Shared spaced
8. Employee Health and Safety
9. Security

PROXIMITY IMPORTANCE

A. Absolutely necessary
E. Especially important
I. Important
O. Ordinary closeness
U. Unimportant
X. Undesirable

Figure 2.20 Example Activity Relationship Profile [25].

INVESTMENT PROFILE

The investment profile indicates the cost and operating parameters necessary to make design and investment decisions. The profile includes the:

- wage rate ($ per hour),

- cost of space ($ per square foot per year),

- cost of capital (% per year),

- required ROI and/or payback period (% or years),

- working days per year (days per year), and

- planning horizon (years).

Design and investment decisions depend heavily on the investment profile. For example, in the auto industry it is not uncommon for warehouse operators to make $30 an hour. It is much easier to justify highly automated systems in that environment than in one where non-union operators are making $7 to $12 per hour. It is much easier to justify high-density storage systems (e.g. vertical carousels, mezzanines, storage drawers, ASRS) when the cost of space is $20-$50 per square foot per year than in the case of a recent project where a 15 year lease was signed for $2.25 per square foot per year. It is much easier to justify highly automated systems when the cost of capital is low (2% to 5%), when the required return-on-investment is low (7% to 12%), and when the required payback period is extended (3-5 years). (We do not run into many of those situations in America. Those economic justification conditions are more common in Japan and parts of Europe. That is why the level of automation in warehousing and distribution in Japan and those parts of Europe is so much higher than that found in the U.S.)

2.8

SUMMARY

By now, I hope you have experienced the power of profiling. If the warehouse activity profile is constructed and presented properly, the design and plan for the warehouse should literally jump off the pages of the profile. In the hands of experienced experts, a thorough profile should and can yield an accurate warehouse concept design in as little as half a day.

If the warehouse activity profile is constructed and presented properly, the design and plan for the warehouse should literally jump off the pages of the profile.

It may appear that profiling is a lot of work. It is! However, it is the work necessary to insure an accurate plan and design for the warehouse. Our clients are often impatient in the profiling phase of a project, anxiously wanting to get to the creative and design phases of the project. Then, once the profile is in place, they often are left with an anticlimactic feeling because the design follows so quickly from the profile.

Remember, there is no other time during the project life cycle - profile, conceptualize, design, implement, and maintain - that design changes are less expensive and the opportunity improvement greater than during the profiling and conceptualizing phases of a project. Once you leave those phases, you need to be completely confident that you have made the right planning and design decisions based on a thorough and objective consideration of the alternatives. Turning back or second guessing at that point is a high penalty to pay for impatience with the profiling process!

WORLD-CLASS WAREHOUSING © EDWARD H. FRAZELLE PH.D.

Finally, some bad news. As soon as the warehouse activity profile has been created, it changes. Hence, once initiated, the profiling process should never end. World-class warehouse management systems support continuous warehouse activity profiling which in turn support continuous warehouse problem solving.

BENCHMARKING WAREHOUSE PERFORMANCE AND PRACTICES

In warehouse activity profiling we diagnosed the problems in the current operations and revealed a variety of opportunities for process improvement. In benchmarking against world-class standards, we set world-class performance, practice, and infrastructure goals for the warehouse operations. The goals have to be set at or above world-class standards since the definition of world-class improves continuously. To set goals below world-class insures that when we get to the goals we set, we will be at least as far behind as we currently are.

The benchmarking and goal setting process described here also permits the quantitative assessment of the opportunity for improvement in productivity, shipping accuracy, inventory accuracy, dock-to-stock time, warehouse order cycle time, and

To set goals below world-class insures that when we get to the goals we set, we will be at least as far behind as we currently are.

storage density. The benchmarking and goal setting process yields an estimate of an annual benefit related to the quantified opportunity for improvement. With that annual benefit ($s per year) in hand, and in relation to the corporate required payback period, an estimate of the affordable investment available for process improvements is easily computed. This estimate further defines the possible alternatives and resources available for process improvements.

Section 1 is an introduction to benchmarking and how it is applied to warehousing and distribution operations. Section 2 describes Warehouse Performance Analysis (WPA), a formal methodology for assessing the performance of warehouse operations in productivity, accuracy, response time, storage density, and level of mechanization. WPA can and should be used for setting project goals, justifying project expenditures, and choosing benchmarking partners. Section 3 presents the warehouse performance index (WPI), a single-score indicator of total warehouse performance. The WPI is related to three key warehouse design factors - workforce demographics, warehouse size, and the level of mechanization.

3.1

INTRODUCTION TO BENCHMARKING WAREHOUSE OPERATIONS

A benchmark is typically a quantitative assessment of some aspect of performance of an enterprise. Benchmarking is the process of gathering and sharing those assessments and developing an improvement plan of action based on the assessment. The process of benchmarking was popularized by the Xerox Corporation in the late 1980s and has been successfully applied to a variety of business functions and industries [2]. The process is a key component of total quality management and there now exists an International Benchmarking Clearinghouse supported by over 100 major corporations [3].

The three perspectives of benchmarking are internal, external, and competitive. Internal benchmarking is focused on the operations of a single company. External benchmarking looks outside the firm's industry. Competitive benchmarking looks at firms conducting business in the same industry. Examples of internal benchmarking, external benchmarking, and competitive benchmarking follow.

INTERNAL BENCHMARKING

I have learned the hard way that the best way to explain benchmarking is through examples. This example of internal logistics benchmarking is from Gillette.

Gillette

Gillette's Latin-American operations include manufacturing and distribution facilities in Mexico, Chile, Brazil, Colombia, Argentina, Venezuela, Ecuador, and Peru. Each year the logistics managers at each operation are measured against 12 key logistics performance indicators including shipping accuracy, inventory accuracy, inventory turns, fill rate, DC productivity, DC storage density, order cycle time, and perfect order percentage. There is a friendly competition among the group for the annual prize in each category and for the overall logistics performance award. Most importantly, the winner in each category is required to teach the group how he or she achieved that success in the previous year. In the course of this process, each operation is improved in every area.

EXTERNAL BENCHMARKING

Excellent examples of external benchmarking from Xerox and Ameritech follow.

Xerox

Xerox Corporation recently embarked on a major distribution network reconfiguration. The reconfiguration included a review of the number, location, and design of all finished goods and service parts distribution facilities. In order to develop highly productive conceptual designs for their distribution centers, Xerox arranged tours of a variety of distribution facilities operating in other industries. During each site visit Xerox and the host company exchanged information concerning the performance and practices of their distribution facilities and discussed the lessons learned by the host company in the design and operation of their facilities. Xerox agreed to host representatives from their benchmarking partners at their new operations once they were complete.

In order to quickly assess the overall performance of each facility on their tour, the logistics engineers from Xerox derived a simple measure of the performance of each distribution facility - the ratio of the annual of lines shipped from the facility to the annual labor hours expended in the facility. Simply, the lines shipped per person-hour. Those facilities with high scores were scrutinized and revisited to insure that the practices in place at those facilities were incorporated in the design of Xerox's new distribution facility.

Because of its excellent customer service and DC operations performance, the focal point for Xerox during the benchmarking exercise became L.L. Bean. Many of the processes in place at L.L. Bean's distribution center were incorporated into the Xerox design. The process worked because today Xerox enjoys a world-class rating in DC operations for service parts and its Chicago service parts DC was recently recognized with *Modern Materials Handling's* annual productivity achievement award [4].

The Xerox case study is a classic example of external benchmarking since Xerox looked outside its own industry for benchmarking partners. That external perspective is critical to the success of the benchmarking exercise. First, most of the breakthroughs in logistics performance and practice have occurred across industry lines. For example, efficient consumer response (ECR) in the grocery industry is a take-off on continuous flow replenishment (CFR) from the electronics industry. CFR is a take-off on quick-response (QR) championed by Milliken in the textiles industry. QR is a take-off on just-in-time (JIT) from the Japanese automotive industry. Another example is the use of carousels in DC operations. Carousels

Most of the break-throughs in logistics performance and practice have occurred across industry lines.

were popularized in dry cleaning and office operations long before they made their way into warehousing. Second, it is typically difficult to gain the necessary cooperation when the partners are within the same industry. Third, by benchmarking just within your own industry, you may establish yourself as the leader in your industry. However, if your industry is not proficient at logistics, you will be the best of a mediocre lot, or as one of my colleagues calls it, the queen of the hogs!

Just as important as the need to benchmark externally is the need to benchmark with *logistically similar* partners. In internal and competitive benchmarking, the similarities are obvious. However, in external benchmarking, it is more difficult to identify logistically similar operations. In the case of Xerox and L.L. Bean, they are logistically similar because their average order value is about the same, their average order cube is about the same, the average number of items on an order is about the same, they handle roughly the same transaction volume, and they carry roughly the same number of SKUs, etc. To the extent your external benchmarking partner is logistically similar to you, your benchmarking partnership will be successful.

Ameritech

Ameritech is one of the nation's largest telecommunications providers located in Chicago, Illinois. Ameritech's Director of Materials Management was recently challenged by the CEO to reduce the cost of logistics in the company by 20% while maintaining and/or improving customer service levels. No additional moneys or resources for additional staff, systems, and/or consultants accompanied the challenge. The director in this case is a very clever gentlemen. He conjectured that many of his colleagues in industry had been given similar charges by their management. He was right!

Ameritech, John Deere, United Stationers, and Exel Logistics recently completed one of the nation's most successful logistics benchmarking partnerships. The partnership was established from the response to invitations sent to companies with reputations for superior warehousing and distribution performance. Companies responding positively to the invitation were reviewed for competitive status, openness to sharing information, logistics similarity, and sensitivity to confidential information. After this filtering step, these four progressive companies were left to the business of distribution performance enhancement.

This process of selecting benchmarking partners was critical to the success of this and to any benchmarking partnership. As Ameritech learned, an excellent benchmarking partner is:

1. Strong in the areas where you are weak and vice-versa.

2. Sensitive to confidentiality requirements.

3. Willing to admit weakness and share lessons learned.

4. Willing to admit strengths and share successes.

5. Open-minded.

6. Logistically similar.

7. Operating in a different industry and perhaps a different country.

The formal benchmarking program began with an initiation meeting at Ameritech's South Bend, Indiana distribution center. During that first meeting the group shared expectations and concerns, toured the DC operations, and developed a questionnaire to facilitate the comparison of the four diverse distribution operations. Each company was allowed to submit 12 questions for the questionnaire. As a result, the questionnaire included 48 questions concerning logistics performance and practices. The next step was the collection and analysis of the questionnaire responses. Since Ameritech called the partnership together, it served as the champion for scheduling meetings and compiling and reporting data.

The team convened three months later at John Deere's top performing distribution operation to review the operations there and to discuss the results of the survey. Next, based on the survey results and a vote of the participating companies, each company was assigned a topic to educate the members on. For example, John Deere's work measurement and safety program is world-renowned. As a result, John Deere was asked to teach the group its capabilities in work measurement and safety. Ameritech's excellence in customer service was readily evident from the survey. It was charged with teaching the group its customer service secrets. United Stationer's productivity was dominant. It was asked to share its productivity secrets. Exel's quality performance stood out and that became the focus of its presentations to the group. Three months later the group convened again at United Stationer's top performing facility to review the operations there and to teach each other their secrets of success and lessons learned. The year-long process brought improved performance for each company as well as life long contacts for each participant in the team.

COMPETITIVE BENCHMARKING

Not long after the merger of two of the nation's largest whole-sale distributors of healthcare supplies, a new vice president of distribution was brought in to oversee the newly merged distribution network. The network included over 30 distribution centers ranging in size from 50,000 to 500,000 square feet. Since the new vice-president was not familiar with the industry's distribution performance, his first management initiative was to commission an assessment of the company's distribution performance as it compared to major competitors. The survey was facilitated by a large consulting organization and included data related to labor productivity measured in units shipped per man-hour, distribution cost as a percentage of sales, inventory turns, accuracy, etc. The results of the survey quickly illustrated the strengths and weaknesses of the company's distribution performance and immediately identified a series of improvement projects.

TRADITIONAL BENCHMARKING PERFORMANCE METRICS

Each of these case studies is an example of how the now common management process called benchmarking is applied in warehousing and distribution. As illustrated in these case studies, the focal point and starting point for the benchmarking process has traditionally been the comparison of quantitative performance measures. For warehousing and distribution functions, the high-profile performance

Warehousing and distribution cost as a percentage of sales varies directly and widely with product pricing and sales volume - aspects of the operation that are usually outside the control of warehouse and distribution management.

dimensions are operating cost, typically measured as warehousing and/or distribution cost as percent of sales, and operating productivity, typically measured in units (lines, orders, cases, pieces, pallets, pounds, etc.) handled per person-hour. (Renewed emphasis on customer service and quality have raised response time and shipping accuracy as critical measures.) Statistics describing performance along those lines are available for a number of key industries [5,6].

Though these measures act as good discussion starters, extreme caution should be used in the interpretation of performance based solely on them. For example, warehousing and distribution cost as a percentage of sales varies directly and widely with product pricing and sales volume - aspects of the operation that are usually outside the control of warehouse and distribution management. Cost as a percentage of sales figures also vary widely across industries. Example industry averages for logistics cost as a percentage of sales are presented in Figure 3.1 below. Warehousing costs can range from 10% to 50% of total logistics cost.

Cost Category	Cost as a % of Sales	Cost per Hundred Weight
Transportation	3.31%	$11.93
Warehousing	2.03%	$10.96
Inventory Carrying	1.82%	$9.86
Customer Service & Order Processing	0.56%	$4.04
Administration	0.39%	$2.13
Other	0.19%	$.66
TOTAL	**7.93%**	**$37.64**

Figure 3.1a Definition and Composition of Logistics Costs [7].

Industry Segment	Logistics Costs as a % of Sales	Logistics Costs per Hundred Weight Shipped
MANUFACTURING	7.77%	$33.36
Industrial Products	7.60%	$39.39
Consumer Goods	7.82%	$31.38
Grocery	7.99%	$15.19
Food & Beverage	8.49%	$8.22
General Merchandise	7.44%	$38.22
Pharmaceuticals	4.31%	$86.00
WHOLESALERS	11.68%	$44.11
RETAILERS	5.34%	$86.15

Figure 3.1b Logistics Costs as a Percentage of Sales for Various Industries [7].

Warehousing unit costs can also be misleading as a performance benchmark. Annual warehousing cost (see Table 3.1) can be easily computed as the sum of the cost of the three major warehouse resources - labor, space, and systems (material handling, storage, and information handling).

Resource	Consumption Measure	Consumption Cost
Labor	Person-Hours per Year	Wage Rate ($ per Person-Hour)
Space	Square Feet Occupied	Cost of Space ($ per Square Foot per Year)
Material and Information Handling Systems	Investment ($s)	Capitalization Rate (% per Year)

Table 3.1 Annual Warehousing Cost Computations.

Annual labor cost is simply the annual hours worked per year multiplied by the wage rate. Annual space cost is the square footage occupied multiplied by the annual cost of space. Annual systems cost is the systems investment cost multiplied by the annual capitalization/depreciation rate.

Again, remember that we are building a report card to assess the management and design of the warehouse. What influence do the managers and designers have on the wage rate? Little or none; the wage rate is a function of the availability of labor in the area and whether the operation is unionized or not. What influence do the managers and designers have on the cost of space? Little or none; the cost of space is a function of the availability of space, the prevailing cost of utilities and insurance. What influence do the managers and designers have on the annual capitalization/depreciation rate? Again, little or none; it is determined by the accountants and financial analysts based on prevailing interest rates and the cost of capital. How well does the annual warehouse operating cost assess the designers and managers of the building as compared with the designers and managers of other operations? Potentially, not very well.

How well does the annual warehouse operating cost assess the designers and managers of the building as compared with the designers and managers of other operations? Potentially, not very well.

Now, consider the resources consumed. How much influence do the designers and managers have over the amount of labor consumed, the amount of space occupied, and the systems investment? A lot! In fact, the design and integration of those resources ultimately determine the performance of the warehouse. The performance in turn determines the cost of the operation. As a result, our benchmarking and goal setting methodology is focused on the consumption of warehouse resources - people, space, and systems - to meet the mission of the warehouse - shipping perfect (right products(s), right quality, on-time, damage-free, right paperwork) orders and storing product efficiently.

In this methodology the warehouse is accountable to the same competitive indicators the business is held to. Businesses compete on the basis of price, quality, and response time. In the warehouse, cost will be our proxy for price, and resource utilization/productivity our proxy for cost. Accuracy will be out proxy for quality. The two key metrics for warehouse accuracy are shipping accuracy and inventory accuracy. Dock-to-stock time and *warehouse order cycle time* (WOCT) will be our proxies for response time. A simple way to remember this is **PAR** - **P**roductivity, **A**ccuracy, and **R**esponse Time!

A simple way to remember this is PAR - Productivity, Accuracy, and Response Time!

It is critical to hold the warehouse accountable to these business measures, since even private warehouses are in effect in business competition with third-party warehousers who are in the business of warehousing. If the private warehousing enterprise is not competitive with potential third-party providers, then the private operator should reconsider its justification for being in the warehousing business. The flip side is that if the private operator is a world-class warehouse operator, then the opportunity is available to turn the warehousing operations into profit-generating third-party operations for the industry and/or other industries. One telecommunications provider has become so dominant in their logistics practices, that it is creating a third-party subsidiary to serve the industry.

Another popular, traditional warehouse performance measure is productivity. The formal definition of productivity is the ratio of the output of an enterprise to the inputs required to achieve that output. In the warehouse, productivity typically refers to labor productivity - the number of units (pounds, lines, order, cases, pallets, etc.) handled divided by the number of person-hours involved. The major misleading factor in this measure is that it only incorporates one of the warehouse resources - labor - and ignores space and systems investments. The indicator can be very misleading. For example, an operation may have a very high labor productivity achieved via inappropriately high investments in material and information handling systems. The focus on a single generic output, units handled, overlooks the other primary missions of a warehouse - storing and accumulating product for shipment.

All of these potential misleading conclusions motivated us to develop warehouse performance analysis (WPA), a benchmarking methodology that assesses the utilization and integration of the warehouse infrastructure - people, space, and systems - to meet the mission of the warehouse - shipping perfect orders on a timely basis and consolidating inventory.

3.2
WAREHOUSE PERFORMANCE ANALYSIS

A recommended set of *warehouse key performance indicators* (WKPIs) is presented in Table 3.2. The table includes the necessary indicators of warehouse infrastructure utilization in meeting the overall mission of the warehouse. The table is not exhaustive and should be tailored for individual operations. To begin to group operations into logistically similar comparisons, the table can be divided into measures for warehouses in which the outbound picking quantities are either broken case quantities, case quantities, or pallet quantities. This is another way of distinguishing logistically similar operations.

Business Metrics	Cost		Quality		Response Time	
Warehouse Metrics	Productivity	Systems Investment	Inbound Accuracy	Outbound Accuracy	Inbound Response Time	Outbound Response Time
Warehouse Key Performance Indicators	Units Handled per Person-Hour	Investment per Square Foot	Inventory Accuracy	Shipping Accuracy	Dock-to-Stock Time	Warehouse Order Cycle Time

Table 3.2 Warehouse Key Performance Indicators (WKPIs)

PRODUCTIVITY

Productivity is measured as the annual lines, cases, or pallets shipped divided by the total annual labor hours employed in the warehouse. The labor hours include operators, supervisors of operators, managers of supervisors, and maintenance and housekeeping personnel. Customer service, inventory administration, sales and marketing, and systems analysis positions are excluded.

WAREHOUSE ACCURACY

Warehouse accuracy indicators include shipping accuracy and inventory accuracy. Shipping accuracy is measured as the percent of lines, cases, or pallets shipped in error relative to the definition of a perfect line item shipment. A line item is shipped perfectly if and only if it is on a perfect order which has the correct quantities, of the correct items, shipped to the correct location, damage-free, on-time, and accompanied by the correct paperwork and/or electronic document. Inventory accuracy is measured as the percent of warehouse locations with an inventory discrepancy.

The best warehouse operators in the U.S. have shipping accuracy at or near 99.97%. The best warehouse operators in Japan have shipping accuracy at or near 99.997%, an order of magnitude improvement. Learning these gaps and experiencing the sense of urgency to close the gap are two of the most valuable results of an external benchmarking process.

WAREHOUSE RESPONSE TIME

Warehouse response time indicators include *dock-to-stock* and *warehouse order cycle time*. The *dock-to-stock* (DTS) stopwatch clicks on when a receipt is on-site and clicks off when the receipt is putaway/cross-docked and made available for picking/shipping. The *warehouse order cycle time* stopwatch clicks on when an order is released to the warehouse floor and clicks off when the order is picked, packed, and ready for shipping.

STORAGE DENSITY

Even in today's low-inventory, just-in-time world, there are good reasons to store product - increasing manufacturing efficiency, positioning product close to key markets, buffering supply and demand schedules, and consolidation for complete order filling. In those cases, *storage density*, measured as the number of pallets, cases, or items housed per square foot is a key warehouse performance indicator. (Ideally we would measure density versus the cube of the warehouse. However, many warehouses do not have the cube calculated.) Unlike productivity and accuracy, where the objective is clearly to maximize the indicator, the storage density should be within a world-class range. Storage density that is too high (greater than 90%) indicates overcrowded conditions and storage density that is too low, (less than 70%) indicates underutilized facilities.

LEVEL OF MECHANIZATION

The level of mechanization is measured as the current replacement cost of all material handling and storage systems (e.g. lift trucks, racking, conveyors, carousels, ASRS machines, etc.) normalized by the square footage in the facility (dollar per square foot). (The investment in warehouse management systems is not included here.) The normalization is necessary to level the playing field for mega-facilities. For example, there are DC operations that occupy more than three million square feet. It would be impossible to operate those facilities without a reasonable level of mechanization, whereas it would be possible to operate fairly small distribution centers and warehouses with little or no mechanization.

The level of mechanization serves as the check and balance for the other indicators. Without including this indicator, a warehouse could overinvest in systems and the scoreboard would not indicate the imbalance.

WAREHOUSE PERFORMANCE ANALYSIS

To help managers and operators assess their own performance relative to world-class standards we developed the warehouse performance analysis chart illustrated in Figure 3.2. The radials (or spokes) represent the key performance indicators for the operations. The outer ring defines world-class performance.

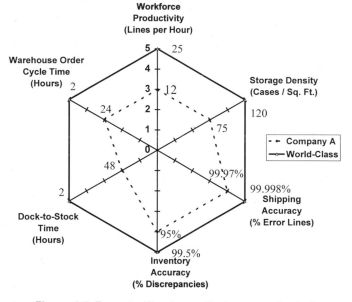

Figure 3.2 Example Warehouse Performance Analysis.

In this example, the warehouse performance indicators are productivity (lines per hour), shipping accuracy (% lines

WORLD-CLASS WAREHOUSING © EDWARD H. FRAZELLE PH.D.

shipped in error), inventory accuracy, dock-to-stock time, warehouse order cycle time, safety, and the level of mechanization. In this particular operation there is $25 invested per square foot to achieve 40 lines per hour, 98% shipping accuracy, 97% inventory accuracy, 8 hours DTS time, 24 hour WOCT, and 30,000 hours worked between recordable accidents. The interpretation is that the operation has not realized the expected return on a relatively high level of investment. (Most U.S. operations have less than $10 invested per square foot.) World-class performance in this industry is 75 lines per hour, 99.998% shipping accuracy, 99.5% inventory accuracy, 2 hours DTS, and 4 hours WOCT.

World-class operators achieve high performance scores with as little mechanization as possible.

Note in the example that a world-class level of mechanization is $0 per square foot. The rationale is that world-class operators achieve high performance scores with as little mechanization as possible. In fact, in many cases they have eliminated the need for mechanization by eliminating much of the work content that might require mechanization. In addition, any investment in mechanization is inherently inflexible.

The value in the gap analysis is the single-page, graphical presentation of the performance profile. The analysis quickly points out weak and strong points in the performance of the operation. The gap chart can also be used to establish project goals. For example, in the figure, the inner ring may represent the current performance of an operation. Another ring may represent the goals of a re-engineering project. The goal ring should be at or near world-class performance. If the goals of a project are not set high enough, since the definition of world-class performance is improving over time, at the completion of the project the operation will not be improved relative to world-class performance.

Another use for the gap chart is in comparing operations in a potential benchmarking partnership. For the partnership to work effectively, the partners should not have overlapping, but offsetting strengths and weaknesses. If the strengths and weaknesses overlap, little learning can take place.

Finally, the gap analysis can also be used in justifying capital expenditures for new information and/or material handling systems. Since the chart quantifies the gap relative to world-class metrics, we can compute the annual dollar benefit (cost savings, cost avoidance, and/or revenue increases) of closing the gap in each performance area. The estimated annual benefit in relation to corporate payback goals suggests an appropriate investment available to close the gap.

The value of the analysis is heavily dependent on the validity of the outer ring. To help operators define these world-class targets, The Logistics Institute at Georgia Tech has developed a database of world-class warehouse performance indicators [6] for a variety of industries. The report is available free of charge from The Logistics Institute at Georgia Tech.

3.3
THE WAREHOUSE PERFORMANCE INDEX

Do you think it would be possible to combine all those performance indicators into a single performance assessment for a warehouse? Another professor and I thought you could. In fact, Dr. Steve Hackman and I worked for two years to combine the performance indicators described above into a single warehouse performance indicator, the *warehouse performance index* (WPI) [8]. The development of the index and related warehouse design and management conclusions are described below.

The WPI is developed with a utility theory technique called *data envelope analysis* (DEA, [8]). The technique is used to compute a productivity index from a series of mission outputs (e.g. orders shipped, material stored, receipts processed) and resource consumptions (e.g. labor hours, square footage, systems investment). An example is provided in Figure 3.3 below.

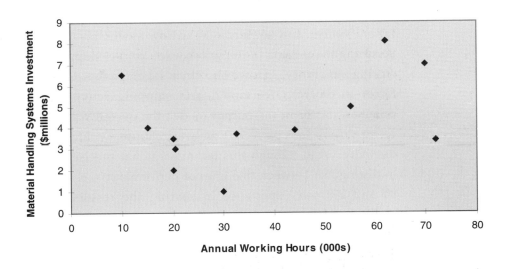

Figure 3.3 Example Data Envelope Analysis Graph.

Imagine that the points on the graph represent warehouses that shipped an identical amount and mix of product last year. Each operation has different values of labor hours consumed and different values of mechanization investment. The operations closest to the origin are the best performers - achieving the same output with fewer resources. The mathematical technique computes the distance of each point from the origin. The operation closest to the origin receives a perfect score of 100. The scores of the other operations are determined based on their distance from the origin relative to the operation with a perfect score.

This example in two-dimensions of resource consumption and one dimension of output is presented to introduce the technique. The DEA methodology allows a multiplicity of resources and a multiplicity of outputs. In our research we explored a wide variety of resource-output models for warehouse operations. The most reliable model centered on the consumption of the three major warehousing resources - labor, space, and material handling systems - used in achieving the mission of the warehouse - perfect shipping and storing inventory. However, since labor is the dominant factor in the resource model, and shipping activity is the dominant factor in the output model, the overall results correlate closely (not perfectly) with warehouse workforce productivity. And, though this technique is not precise enough to distinguish between fine lines of performance (i.e. between 85 and 87) our experience in sharing the results with a number of companies suggests that the technique is adequate for overall warehouse performance assessments (i.e. excellent, good, average, poor).

Just being able to assign a performance score to a warehouse is useful to identify the application of best-practices. However, the ability to in turn review the performance scores and their relation with key design factors is invaluable for insights into the application and integration of the key warehouse resources - labor, space, and systems.

WORKFORCE DEMOGRAPHICS AND WAREHOUSE PERFORMANCE

A wide range of human resource data was collected at each facility including wage rates, the number of direct and indirect positions and hours involved in each warehousing function, the average education achieved by warehouse operators, and union composition. Of particular interest was the correlation between the computed warehouse performance index and the presence or absence of unions. Interestingly, our observations are split nearly evenly between union and non-union operations. Would you expect that union or non-union operations would have a higher average performance score?

The average performance index for union facilities was nearly identical to that of the non-union facilities. In reviewing our observation and interview notes, we observed that union operations that exhibited high performance all made strategic use of management tactics to automatically pace the flow of work. Those tactics included:

· time standards and incentives to motivate high productivity;

· radio frequency terminals and light-directed picking to establish continuous, real-time monitoring of transactions; and

· automated material handling systems to machine-pace the work flow and facilitate supervision.

In reviewing our observation and interview notes, we observed that union operations that exhibited high performance all made strategic use of management tactics to automatically pace the flow of work.

Ford and Chrysler Service Parts

At Ford and Chrysler all of these techniques have been combined at their service parts distribution centers. All of their U.S. service parts distribution centers have been reconfigured around carousel-driven, light-directed order picking. In each operation, an order picker is assigned to a pod of three horizontal carousels - left, center, and right. While the order picker is picking from one carousel, the other two carousels are rotating to the next pick location. As a result, the order picker is never traveling and never idle waiting on a carousel. A vertical light display in front of each carousel indicates and directs the order picker to pick the correct quantity from the correct location. With parts in hand, the order picker turns to sort the parts into customer order totes. The totes are in light-directed flow racks located directly behind the operator. The correct sortation of the parts into customer order totes is directed by a horizontal light display on the flow rack.

In this operating scenario the carousels eliminate traveling, help to pace the work, and facilitate supervision since all the operators should be aligned at their order picking stations. The picking and sortation lights also help to pace the flow of work and provide transaction times for operator productivity tracking. Time standards and incentives, based on productivity tracking data provided by the light-directed systems, also serve to increase productivity.

In retrospect, these management techniques all have something in common - they automate and facilitate the supervision of the workforce - one of the keys to effectively managing a union or any workforce.

WORLD-CLASS WAREHOUSING © EDWARD H. FRAZELLE PH.D.

WAREHOUSE SIZE AND WAREHOUSE PERFORMANCE

Do you think large or small warehouses tend to have better performance?

A variety of data points was used to assess the scale of each warehouse operation including annual throughput, number of items housed in the warehouse, number of shipping and receiving docks, annual sales, and total floorspace measured in square footage. In no case were we able to make a definitive statement concerning the quantifiable relationship between the scale of warehouse operations and warehouse performance. However, based on the results displayed in Figure 3.4, there appears to be very little support for the theory of strong economies of scale in warehousing and distribution operations.

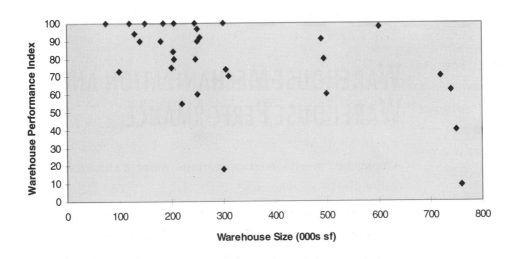

Figure 3.4 Warehouse Performance Index vs. Warehouse Size [8].

In large facilities, the inherent productivity hurdles of excessive travel distances, poor work flow visibility, and difficult communication and supervision appear to offset any economies brought on by increased order volumes or high levels of mechanization. In large facilities the travel time penalties for improper slotting, order batching, or task sequencing seem to grow exponentially with the size of facility. For example, in one two million square foot distribution center the productivity penalties for improper slotting, batching, and sequencing result in an annual walking budget for the warehouse of over $3 million.

The size of the warehouse also tends to increase the span of control. The greater the span of control, the more skilled the managers and supervisors need to be. Unfortunately, there is a severe shortage in the number of highly skilled warehouse operations managers and supervisors. As a result, as a warehouse grows, the management requirements can quickly exceed the management and supervisory capability.

Based on our analysis and confirmed in a variety of project settings, we can not assume that a high degree of mechanization will yield a high warehouse performance (see Figure 3.5).

WAREHOUSE MECHANIZATION AND WAREHOUSE PERFORMANCE

Are highly mechanized operations more productive than conventional warehouses?

Based on our analysis and confirmed in a variety of project settings, we can not assume that a high degree of mechanization will yield a high warehouse performance (see Figure 3.5). In fact, a high degree of mechanization may yield just the opposite effect. How could that happen? Excess complexity, inadequate or no training, ill-advised experimentation, subjective decision making, improper financial justification, and inflexibility are just some of the ways.

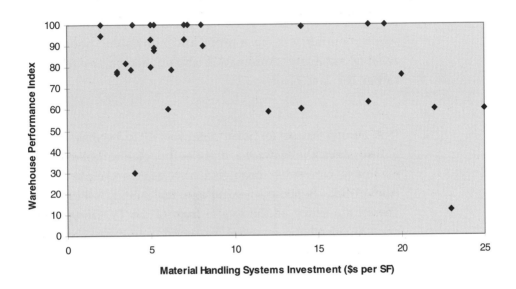

Figure 3.5 Warehouse Performance Index vs. Level of Mechanization [8].

Do's and Don'ts for Warehouse Automation

This list of do's and don'ts will help you avoid some of the potential pitfalls of warehouse automation and mechanization.

Complexity

We often believe automation is a way to streamline a complex process, manage a complex process, and/or make a complex process more efficient. Instead, automation is inherently complex. By applying complexity to a complex situation we get complexity squared! The correct approach is to simplify and streamline a process first - taking as much work content out as possible. At that point, there may not be enough work content left to automate; and/or what remains will be simple and consistent enough to reliably automate. Automation should not be the first but rather the last resort.

Don't assume automation can resolve a complex situation. Do simplify first.

It is human nature (or what has evolved to become human nature since the dawning of sales people) to believe that machines can solve problems. A classic example is the NordicTrack. Suppose I need to lose ten pounds (which I do). There I am sitting on the sofa in front of the TV eating potato chips. Guess what commercial comes on? You guessed right, the NordicTrack commercial with super-fit models gliding along and losing pounds right there in front of my eyes. The 1-800 number comes on the screen. All I need is a credit card. Voila! I am ten pounds lighter — in my dreams. In fact, if it was that easy, I would lose the ten pounds when they debited my credit card.

Unfortunately, it doesn't work that way. I have to assemble the machine, read the instructions, and worse yet follow a regimented program of disciplined exercise and performance monitoring. Even worse, I have to diet and keep track of my eating to make all this work. All of a sudden I have discovered the truth.

What makes a difference is my behavior and disciplines, not the machine. In fact, the machine is only a tool. If I do not use it properly, it will not be helpful and may even cause injury. Get the point? The situation is the same with a carousel, new order picker truck, new warehouse management system, or any other new system.

Don't take training and documentation for granted. Do appropriate the necessary training and documentation time and budget.

Training and Documentation

We recently worked with a client on the west coast that installed a $3 million warehousing system including light-directed carousels, wave picking and automated sortation, and a supporting warehouse management system. Unfortunately, all of the WKPIs - productivity, accuracy, response time - are worse now than they were before the system was installed. The major reason for the system failure is the absence of any training or system documentation. In the heated bidding competition the low bidder secured the position by removing training and documentation from their proposal, and they never made it back in. Now, would you as the project champion be willing to go back to the board of directors and ask for the additional $300,000 required to train the affected people and document the systems? I hope so. But in this instance, the project champion will not take that step. Until he does, the company will continue to own and operate a Masserati without an owner's manual and without a driving course.

The Guinea Pig

Don't be the guinea pig. Do see and evaluate the proposed system in a live setting.

I recently took a call from the head legal counsel for a large snack foods company. The counsel indicated that his company wanted to bring a lawsuit against a material handling supplier whose wire-guided order picker trucks would not run in reverse. They wanted to bring a lawsuit to reclaim productivity damages.

As usual I started to ask questions about the circumstances surrounding the case. First, I asked if the design team had ever seen this sort of system in operation. Counsel indicated they had. Next, I asked where they had seen it. Counsel indicated that the team visited one of the beta-site installations. Unfortunately the system was not operating that day, but they had seen a video where the system was really working well. What can I say? Next Case!

Cross-Functional Teams

Don't justify and design the system in a vacuum. Do use a cross-functional team including operations, engineering, customer service, and systems on the team.

I was involved in a recent project in which the project team was dominated by a boisterous former military logistician. He quickly became known as Captain Carousels since no matter what the analysis indicated, no matter what the wishes of the group were, no matter, no matter, no matter, according to him we were going to have carousels in his warehouse. Whether convinced by a clever sales person, captivated by an advertisement and/or case study in a magazine, or whether from past experience, Captain Carousels was one big obstacle that had to be overcome. If he were allowed to act independently, you can only imagine the outcome. Unfortunately, it happens.

One of my business partners always says that, "People will only successfully implement what they design themselves." It is true. If the cross-functional team designs the solution, then for their own self-preservation, they will make it work.

Incremental Justification

Imagine that a material handling or warehouse management systems supplier brings a project to you that costs $1 million and can yield $1 million in annual cost savings. The one year payback seems attractive. All systems go, right? Wrong! In this case, the $1 million in annual savings is the yield relative to the current, lousy situation. Many millions of capital dollars have been justified against a current lousy situation. The correct approach is to consider the investment relative to the current situation modified by very inexpensive process improvements. Then the improved state becomes the right backdrop against which to consider the large initial investment. For example, in warehousing, many of the WKPIs can be improved through improved slotting, order batching, picking tour construction, and work flow simplification. These improvements typically yield a 20% to 30% improvement in overall warehouse productivity, yet they can be realized with a small initial investment. After these improvements have been made, a large investment can be considered. In the case of the $1 million we were considering relative to a $1 million annual savings, the true annual savings may only be $250,000. In that case the payback period is 4 years. That may or may not be justifiable. Either way, it is the correct financial assessment, and the process improvements that were made will increase the likelihood of success for the investment project. This approach to project justification is called *incremental justification* (see Figure 3.6).

Don't accept the justification of the new system relative to the existing situation. Do incrementally justify the project relative to an improved current situation.

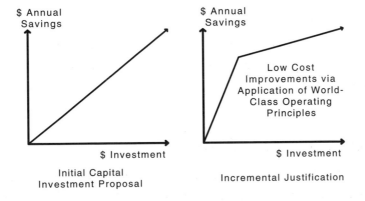

Figure 3.6 Incremental Justification Approach.

Admittedly, there are situations when a capital investment is made solely with infrastructure, competitive, and/or customer service justifications. In those cases, the project should be labeled as such and audited as such.

Flexibility

Highly mechanized systems are typically difficult to reconfigure. For example, a consumer electronics company recently designed, purchased, and installed an automated storage and retrieval system for pallet handling. Six months after the system was installed the order patterns changed dramatically, requiring case-as opposed to pallet-quantity customer shipments. Since the pallet handling system was not conducive to case picking, and since the highly automated system was nearly impossible to reconfigure, the company was forced to either suffer the productivity penalty in working around the new system or initiate the design of an entirely new system.

Don't assume a higher level of mechanization will bring increased flexibility. Do consider that higher levels of mechanization bring flexibility risk.

WAREHOUSE PRACTICES AND WAREHOUSE PERFORMANCE

After presenting all of this analysis I am often asked what separates world-class performers from the rest of the pack. The major distinguishing feature of world-class performing warehouses is their practices. You often hear basketball or football coaches say that their team performs the way they practice. It is the same in warehousing. The warehouse performs as a function of its practices. In other words, the performance indicators, good or bad, are a direct result of the design and management of the underlying processes in the warehouse. We often look for excuses such as a lack of resources, the burden of the union, the attitude of the executives, etc. The truth is in the processes, polices, and procedures that are carried out inside the four walls of the warehouse.

To help people evaluate their warehousing practices we developed a warehouse practices gap analysis similar in concept to the warehouse performance analysis. The major difference is that practice descriptions are not quantifiable. Instead, for each functional area in the warehouse (receiving, putaway, storage, replenishment, slotting, order picking, shipping, communications, work measurement) we describe world-class (stage 5), middle-class (stage 3), and no-class (stage 1) practices (see Figure 3.7).

For example, no-class receiving would proceed as follows: When a receipt shows up, we have no idea it is coming. We have no idea what is in the receipt and if and/or when we ordered it. Since we have no idea the receipt is coming, there is no crew available to unload the truck and potentially no dock available. When a crew and/or dock is available we open the door, unload the receipt, and stage it at the dock. Finally, we have somebody pull some paperwork on the receipt, match it with a purchase order and correct the purchase orders (assuming the receipts we found are right). Then, we ask a lift truck operator to put the loads away, one at a time, finding the nearest open location or aisle for the loads and memorizing the putaway location(s). It is getting a little ridiculous, right? Unfortunately, this ridiculous example hits very close to home for some operators.

The performance indicators, good or bad, are a direct result of the design and management of the underlying processes in the warehouse.

	Stage 1	Stage 2	Stage 3	Stage 4	Stage 5
	Unload, Stage, & In-Check	Immediate Putaway to Reserve	Immediate Putaway To Primary	Cross-Docking	Pre-Receiving
Putaway	First-Come-First-Serve	Batched By Zone	Batched & Sequenced	Location-to Stocker	Automated Putaway
Reserve Storage	Floor Storage	Convencional Racking & Bins	Some Double Deep Storage	Some Narrow Aisle Storage	Optimal Hybrid Storage
Picking	Pick-to-Single-Order	Batch Picking	Zone Picking-Progressive Assembly	Zone Picking-Downstream Sorting	Dynamic Picking
Slotting	Random	Popularity Based	Popularity and Cube Based	Popularity, Cube and Correlation Based	Dynamic Slotting
Replenishment	As Needed-Pick Face Complete	As Needed Downtream Complete	Anticipated - by Sight	Anticipated-Automated	Pick from Reserve Storage
Shipping	Check, Stage, & Load	Stage & Load	Direct Load	Automated Loading	Pick-to-Trailer
Work Measurement	No Standards	Standards Used for Planning	Standards Used for Evaluation	Standards Used for Incentive Pay	Standards Used for Continuous Feedback
Communications	Paper	Bar Code Scanning	RF Terminals	Handsfree	Virtual Displays

Figure 3.7 World-Class Warehousing Practices.

Burlington Industries

Now, to stage 5, world-class receiving. At Burlington Industries, pallet loads coming off of manufacturing lines are loaded directly onto outbound trailers for shipping. Each pallet has a bar-coded license plate, which a lift truck operator scans as he picks the load up at the end of the manufacturing line. As the lift truck operator takes the load onto the outbound trailer, he scans a bar code label above the shipping door to log the load onto the outbound load. When all the loads have been positioned on the trailer, the load is closed out and an *advance shipping notice* (ASN) is forwarded to the customer indicating the time the load is leaving, the exact position of each pallet on the truck, and the scheduled arrival time.

In addition, each outbound trailer has a RF tag imbedded in the windshield. As the truck makes its way toward the customer location, antennae located every 10 miles along the highway read the tag as the truck goes by to update the customer's system with the location and expected arrival time. Since the receipt was scheduled by the customer, a dock door and crew are pre-assigned to the load. As each pallet is unloaded at the dock, the license plate is scanned, for an inquiry on the disposition of the load. The first check is for cross-docking. If the item is required for an outstanding order, the lift truck operator is directed to take the load to the trailer where that load is being prepared. Otherwise, the lift truck operator is directed to a pre-assigned location (assigned by the warehouse management system during the in-transit time) for the item. The first choice is a primary pick location if it needs restocking, then the reserve location.

Now, compare the amount of material handling and elapsed time in each example. The key to improving warehouse performance is reducing the work content, primarily material and information handling. Every time a piece of material or paper is handled, the amount of time and resources required to do the job increase. Also, every time a piece of material or information is handled, the likelihood of error increases.

To help people benchmark their practices against world-class, we created a methodology similar to warehouse

As the truck makes its way toward the customer location, antennae located every 10 miles along the highway read the tag as the truck goes by to update the customer's system as to the location and expected arrival time.

performance analysis. As you may have guessed it is called warehouse practices gap analysis. An example is illustrated below (see Figure 3.8). Each of the radials represents one of the functional areas in the warehouse. As before, the outer ring defines world-class standards. The practices of the warehouse are then plotted relative to the world-class definitions provided earlier. As before, this technique can be used to set project goals, to assess benchmarking partners, and in this particular example to conduct a functional evaluation of a warehouse management system.

The key to improving warehouse performance is reducing the work content, primarily material and information handling.

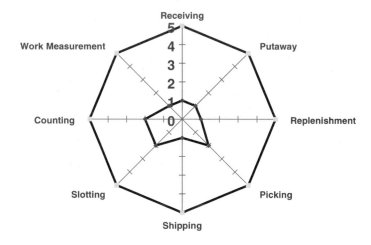

Figure 3.8 Example Warehouse Practices Gap Analysis.

3.4
SUMMARY

1. Benchmarking is a critical step on the way to world-class warehousing.

2. External benchmarking should be used to set world-class goals for the warehouse operations and process improvement projects.

3. The benchmarking process should jointly consider all the major warehouse performance indicators including productivity, shipping accuracy, inventory accuracy, dock-to-stock time, warehouse order cycle time, and the level of mechanization.

4. Benchmarking and warehouse performance gap analysis should be used to incrementally justify capital expenditures.

5. Benchmarking and warehouse practices analysis should be used to align the warehouse practices with world-class standards.

SIMPLIFYING WAREHOUSE OPERATIONS

Another critical step on the way to world-class warehousing is to simplify the warehouse operations by aligning the processes with world-class warehouse operating principles. Those principles are all designed to do the same thing: eliminate and streamline work content. Work content in a warehouse or distribution center is material and/or information handling. Think of it this way. If you took the roof off your warehouse and looked down from a helicopter, what would you see the people in the warehouse doing? That's right, for the most part they are traveling to, from, and between warehouse locations. (A typical distribution of a warehouse operator's time is presented in Figure 4.1). To make real progress in simplifying and streamlining the warehouse operations, the traveling and material handling must be eliminated and/or reduced.

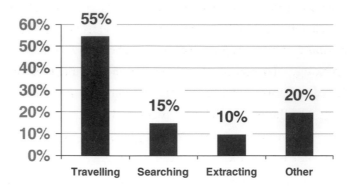

Figure 4.1 Typical Distribution of a Warehouse Operator's Time.

These principles are also written from the perspective of attacking the most costly, time consuming, and error-ridden function in the warehouse - order picking. A typical functional distribution of the cost of operating a warehouse is presented in Figure 4.2.

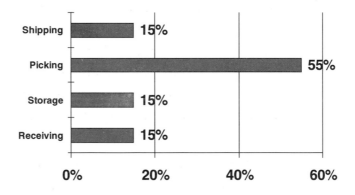

Figure 4.2 Typical Functional Distribution of Warehouse Operating Costs.

Note that order picking makes up the majority of operating cost. You may recall that the three major resources in warehousing are people, space, and systems. As a result, it should not be a surprise that order picking represents such a large portion of the warehouse operating costs. Order picking is the most labor intensive function in the warehouse. It is not unusual to find a majority of the warehouse workforce in order picking. To combat the labor intensity, most of the material and information handling systems in warehousing are devoted to the order picking function. In addition, many of the decision support systems and engineering projects in a warehouse are associated with order picking. Finally, many of the errors made in warehousing are made in the order picking function. Hence, order picking is often the major source of the cost of warehousing errors.

With all of these resources devoted to order picking, with perfect order filling being one of the two missions of any warehouse, and with all of the customer service ramifications of the order picking process, I have personally devoted more than ten years of research and project work to making the order picking process less time consuming, less costly, and more accurate. In so doing, I have learned that the application of these seven operating principles, originally designed to improve order picking, yield dramatic improvements in all the key warehouse performance indicators and in every functional area in the warehouse.

The application of these seven operating principles, originally designed to improve order picking, yield dramatic improvements in all the key warehouse performance indicators and in every functional area in the warehouse.

The principles are presented in a sequence to correspond with one of Drucker's Laws, "Some people are paid to do things right. Others are paid to do the right things." We are paid to do both. In this case, the right thing to do is to eliminate as much work content as possible. From the standpoint of order picking, that means eliminating it. After we have applied the principles aimed at eliminating order picking altogether, we will work to make the remaining work content as efficient as possible.

DIRECT SHIPPING AND CROSS-DOCKING

What is the highest order picking productivity could be? 100 lines per person-hour? No, I have seen operations where the order picking productivity is more than 2,000 lines per person-hour. Is that the highest? No. In fact, there can be infinite productivity in order picking. Recall the definition of labor productivity. The numerator is the output, lines or units picked; the denominator is the input, person-hours. This ratio could be infinity if the denominator goes to zero. In other words, if we could somehow get the picking work done without having anyone employed in order picking, then we could achieve infinite order picking productivity.

Sounds great! Is it possible? Absolutely. There are two possibilities. The first is to completely automate the picking process. Believe it or not, there are large case picking operations in Japan in which no human touches a pallet or a case, from receiving to shipping. In Germany there are broken case picking operations in which no human touches the product. In these operations the order picking productivity is indeed infinity. Unfortunately, the investment required is nearly infinity as well. Better than completely automating the order picking process is to completely eliminate it via direct shipping and/or cross-docking.

In *direct shipping*, product is shipped directly from the source of supply to the customer. For example, at L.L. Bean, the canoes and large items that come to your door are not housed in the L.L. Bean distribution center. They are shipped directly to your door from the manufacturing facility. Since the items never arrive at the DC, they do not have to be unloaded, staged, put away, replenished to a forward pick location, picked, packed, checked, staged, and loaded. Consider all of the work, time, and potential for error that is eliminated as a result. Every justifiable direct shipment should be aggressively pursued! Opportunities for direct shipping include large, bulky items; made-to-order items; and combinations of items for which the regular shipping volume occupies at least a full truckload.

After direct shipping, the next most attractive warehousing practice is *cross-docking*. Cross docking is the practice of moving product from receiving immediately to shipping for loading into a customer order. In so doing, the traditional warehouse processes of receiving staging, receiving putaway, storage, pick line replenishment, and picking are eliminated. Again, consider all of the work, time, and potential for error that is eliminated as a result. As was the case with direct shipping, we would like to take advantage of this practice whenever possible. Three cross-docking examples are described below.

AMWAY

Amway is a major manufacturer and direct-to-consumer distributor of consumer and personal products including soaps, cleaning supplies, and cosmetics. At its central distribution center in Ada, Michigan, receipts from manufacturing are scheduled and all incoming pallets have bar code license plates. As a lift truck operator unloads a trailer, a pallet license plate (bar code) is scanned to inform the warehouse management system that the pallet is on-site. The warehouse management system then directs the operator to move the pallet to its assigned warehouse location. The first priority for the pallet is cross-docking. In fact, if the item is required in an outstanding order that is currently being loaded (and if there is no violation of code-date expiration windows for pallets in inventory of the same item) the operator is directed to move (cross-dock) the pallet to that dock for shipping. The next priority is *direct-putaway* to a primary pick location. This transaction is recommended if there is an opening for the pallet in the primary pick location. The last priority is to move the pallet to its reserve warehouse location. Even in that case, there is no staging of the product since locations are either pre-assigned or assigned in real-time. (Some warehouses are purposefully designed without receiving staging space to discourage any receiving staging.)

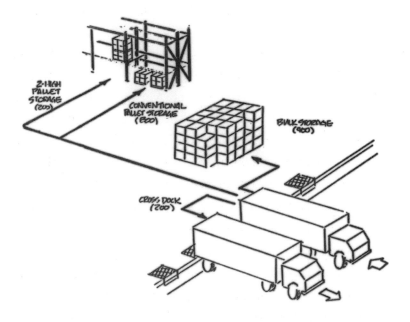

Figure 4.3 Typical Cross-Docking Configuration [Apple].

K-Mart

At K-Mart's jewelry distribution center, suppliers are required to bar code license plate each carton. At the receiving dock, inbound cartons are properly oriented and manually off-loaded onto a telescoping conveyor. The telescoping conveyor feeds a sortation conveyor just inside the doors of the DC. A bar code scanner located on the conveyor reads the carton license plate to make the real-time warehouse management system aware that the carton is on-site. In turn, the warehouse management system directs the conveyor to direct the carton to the cross-docking operation (if there is an outstanding open order for the item) or to the traditional store, pick, pack, and ship operation.

In the cross-docking operation, each K-Mart store has a tote position in one of six carousels. As an inbound carton is presented to a carousel operator, the operator is directed by a CRT and a light tree to distribute the contents of the carton to the stores in the carousel carrier in front of the operator. The contents of the carton are depleted this way. When a store order is complete, a flashing light display indicates that the corresponding order is complete. The operator pushes the tote through the back of the carousel where a takeaway conveyor takes the tote to shipping. More than 50% of the merchandise in the DC is cross-docked in this manner.

These are good examples of cross-docking for full pallets and loose cartons. In general, what types of unit loads are good candidates for cross-docking? As these examples suggest, full pallets with a single SKU on-board are good candidates since the pallet does not have to be decomposed, the entire pallet is cross-docked, and the entire pallet can be automatically identified with a bar code license plate. Floor-loaded loose cartons are also good candidates for the same reasons - the carton does not have to be decomposed, the entire carton is cross-docked, and the carton can be automatically identified with a bar code license plate. Mixed SKUs on a pallet or mixed SKUs in a carton are difficult for cross-docking since the contents of the unit load must be sorted before an operator or conveyor can be directed to cross-dock the merchandise. By the time the contents of the unit load have been sorted out, the time window for effective cross-docking has typically passed.

The other natural scenarios for cross-docking are:

- backorders since there is by definition an outstanding order for those products on backorder,

- made-to-order products since by definition there is an outstanding order for those products when they hit the receiving dock,

- customer-ready-product customized by the supplier, and

- branch and inter-DC transfers.

SPARTAN STORES

Direct shipping and cross-docking are so effective that entire industries are taking steps to maximize the application of these principles. For example, the logistics of efficient consumer response (ECR) makes direct shipping and cross-docking the foundation of physical distribution in the grocery industry. A classic example is from Spartan Stores, a $2 billion grocer headquartered in Grand Rapids, Michigan. There the A movers (based on cube-movement) are shipped in truckload quantities from food manufacturers to grocery retail stores. B movers are precisely scheduled into a central DC for daily cross-docking to build consolidated (frozen, refrigerated, and ambient temperature) loads for retail stores. C movers are stored in a contiguous DC specially designed for dense storage and batch picking of slow moving items. A daily batch is picked of the C items and inducted into the cross-docking operation. (Of course to take advantage of this operating philosophy, the warehouse activity profiling is critical and must be done continuously.)

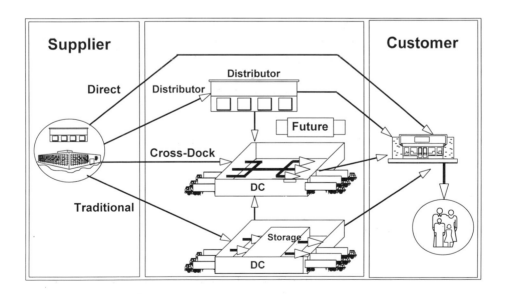

Figure 4.4 Cross-docking Concept for the Food Industry [24].

PRE-PACKAGING

If there are 100 cartons on a pallet, and a customer orders 100 cartons, would you rather pick a full pallet, or handle 100 individual cartons? You did not need to buy this book to learn that it requires much less time and work to handle the full pallet. The same could be said for a full case as opposed to breaking a case open for order picking, or for a full truckload container as opposed to loose pallets on a LTL shipment.

Not only would we rather handle a full, as opposed to a partial unit load at a time, but our customer would as well. It is much easier for our customer to handle a full truckload as opposed to a partial truckload, a full pallet as opposed to loose cartons, and a full case as opposed to a broken case.

NASHUA

Nashua Corporation is a large manufacturer of computer and office supplies. Its warehouse activity profile indicated that customers tend to order quarter, half, and full pallet quantities. Yet, they did not have any quarter and half pallet quantities pre-configured. In this case, the DC is attached to manufacturing. Hence, we need only direct the palletizer to create the appropriate mix of full, half, and quarter pallet quantities. Then, we need to let the customer service group know about the unit load configurations so they can encourage customers to order in the preconfigured increments. In this case, the head of sales and marketing was on the design team and he instituted the new policy the next week. (Other options for pre-configuring partial unit loads include having the supplier do it and/or configuring the loads at receiving.)

The same concept can apply in broken case picking, in which customers often order in common increments. Examples are quarter and half case quantities, and numerical increments of 5, 10, 20, 25, 50, 100, etc. Again, those are opportunities for pre-packaging on-site at receiving or at the supplier's site. In either case, the practice reduces the work, time, and likelihood of error in the order filling process.

4.3
PICK FROM STORAGE

The traditional U-shape warehouse layout (Figure 4.5) and process incorporates receiving docks, receiving staging, receiving inspection, putaway to reserve storage, reserve pallet storage and pallet picking, case pick line replenishment from pallet storage, case picking, broken case pick line replenishment from case storage, broken case picking, packing, accumulation, shipping staging, and shipping docks.

Why do we need so many different storage and picking areas? Why do we need separate forward areas for case and broken case picking? The reason is that broken and full-case picking productivity from a large reserve pallet storage is

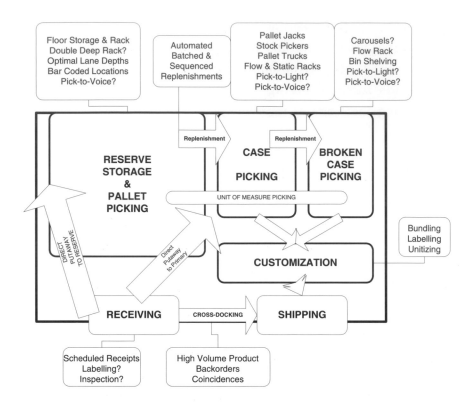

Figure 4.5 Traditional U-shape Warehouse Configuration.

unacceptably low. The forward areas are small and compact, are uniquely configured for the picking task, and may have specialized equipment. As a result, the picking productivity in these areas is 10 to 20 times what the productivity would be in a large reserve storage area where the entire inventory for a single item would be housed. The picking productivity gain is almost always so great (as compared to picking from reserve storage locations) that the cost penalties paid for replenishing the forward areas, and the space penalty paid for establishing these stand alone areas is rarely considered.

Now, suppose we could achieve forward picking rates from a reserve storage area? In so doing, we can have our cake and eat it too - excellent picking productivity, no forward area replenishment, and no extra space set aside for forward areas. Is it possible? It is in Ford's service parts distribution centers.

FORD SERVICE PARTS

At Ford's service parts distribution centers (see Figure 4.6), receipts arrive by rail in wire baskets, each identified with a bar code license plate. The wire baskets are moved by a lift truck operator to an automated receiving station. At the receiving station the receiving operator scans the bar code to let the warehouse management system know that the item and cage are on-site. The system then directs the operator to distribute the contents of the cage into one or more tote pans, each with a bar code license plate. Each tote is in turn assigned to and conveyed to one of 54 horizontal carousels for putaway by the carousel operator. The carousel operators each work a pod of three carousels. A real-time warehouse management system interleaves the putaway and picking tasks. All picking is light-directed and the operator is also light-directed to distribute each pick into order totes housed in flow racks adjacent to the carousels. 80% of all part numbers and a corresponding portion of the activity in the DC is handled this way.

Is this picking from storage? Yes, because the 54 carousels act as the reserve storage area. The entire inventory for an item is housed in the carousel system, but not necessarily in the same carousel location. There is no replenishment within the system and there is no space set aside for back-up stock.

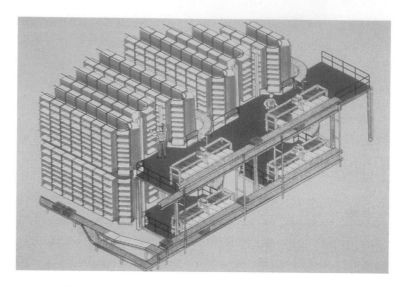

Figure 4.6 Pick-from-Storage Order Picking Concept.

This operating concept gives Ford a significant competitive advantage in service parts logistics. The concept requires a highly sophisticated logistics information system (random storage, intelligent slotting, activity balancing, dynamic wave planning), a high degree of mechanization (to move the reserve storage locations to the order picker), and a disciplined workforce. This operating philosophy is not meant for every situation, but when the operating volumes are large enough, and the necessary resources are available, the pick-from-storage concept can yield tremendous productivity gains.

4.4
WORK SIMPLIFICATION

After applying the first three principles the opportunities for order of magnitude improvements are exhausted. The remaining four warehouse operating principles are designed to yield 20% to 50% perfomance improvements. We will begin by eliminating and combining the tasks of the warehouse operators. A list of the typical set of tasks for a warehouse operator is presented in Table 4.1 below. Adjacent to each task is one or more strategies for eliminating the task. The table can and should be used as a checklist for performance improvement opportunities.

By applying these first four principles we have eliminated as much of the warehousing work content as is feasible and justifiable. The next three operating principles need to be applied to the remaining work content to make it as efficient as possible. These principles are interdependent and define the overall operating philosophy of a warehouse or distribution center. The three principles relate to slotting, batching, and sequencing.

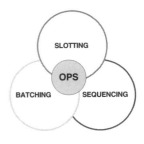

Slotting determines for each item in the warehouse (1) its appropriate storage **mode**, (2) its appropriate **allocation of space** in the mode, and (3) its **exact location** within the mode. Good slotting practice maximizes picking productivity and storage density by perfectly assigning items to their proper storage modes, their proper amount of space in the mode, and their proper location in the storage mode. Slotting depends on the way orders and putaways are batched together and the manner in which operators are sequenced along the pick line.

Batching determines the assigned workset for each pick, or putaway, or pick face replenishment. For example, orders may be batched together to make efficient picking tours or to make waves for specific carriers departing the warehouse. Picks and putaways may be batched together (or *interleaved*)

Task	Strategies to Eliminate
1 Traveling to, from, and between warehouse locations.	. Bring the putaway/picking location to the operator (i.e. carousels, automated storage and retrieval systems).
2. Searching for warehousing locations.	. Bring the location to the operator. . Use lights to illuminate the correct location. . Use RF terminals and/or voice headsets to direct the operator.
3. Taking cases or loose items out of warehouse locations.	. Automated dispensing systems - A-frames and V-frames for loose items, automated case pickers for case picking.
4. Count.	. Weigh counting . Prepackaging in increments that customers are likely to order in.
5. Retrieve, read, and file paperwork.	. Paperless warehousing systems. . RF Terminals. . Pick-to-light systems. . Voice headsets.
6. Write.	. Data entry via scanning, keypad entry, voice i/o, and/or pick-to-light indicators.
7. Setup picking tours (i.e. organize vehicle and paperwork for picking).	. Pre-setup to avoid disrupting the picking process. Like truckers should keep on trucking; pickers should keep on picking.
8. Restock empty pick locations (or pick locations with an insufficient pick quality to fill the cuantity requested on the order).	. Automated look ahead replenishment should insure that each location has a sufficient pick quantity before the order picker reaches the location.
9. Checking and verifying.	. Pick by location and weigh check downstream from picking.
10. Loading/unloading	. Automated loading and unloading devices and robotic loading/unloading systems can be used to eliminate manual loading and unloading.
11. Idling waiting for work.	. A real-time warehouse management system should keep a perpetual do-list of transactions. Dynamic wave planning and dynamic zone sizing can also eliminate idling.
12. Excessive socializing and congestion.	. Assign operators to dedicated zones for picking and putaway.

Table 4.1 Warehousing Tasks and Strategies to Eliminate Them.

to make picking and putaway travel tours. In either case, the objective of batching is to maximize operating productivity by reducing travel times and balancing workloads. Batching decisions depend on the way the warehouse is slotted.

Sequencing orders the transactions within a batch of work. For example, once a group of orders is batched together to form a picking tour, the picks in the tour should be presented to the order picker in warehouse location sequence. The orders in a pick wave may be sequenced by the departure time of their associated carrier. In either case, the sequencing decision depends on the way work is batched together and on the way the warehouse is slotted.

These three operating decisions combined define the operating philosophy of any warehouse or distribution center and govern the overall performance of the operations. As a result, what should be three critical evaluation criteria for any warehouse management system? That's right - the way the system performs slotting, batching, and sequencing. These three decision operations applied to the main documents of the warehouse -purchase orders and customer orders - should be the foundation of any warehouse management system. From that core functionality should come the functionality for receiving, putaway, storage, picking, and shipping.

Unfortunately, many warehouse management systems were not and are not built around these three decisions. Instead, they have evolved from other applications including manufacturing, inventory management, finance, and/or customer service. The typical construction of these systems is functional (as opposed to algorithmical). In other words, system modules are created for each functional area in the warehouse - receiving, receiving inspection, putaway, storage, pick line replenishment, order picking, and shipping. These modules may or may not be written by the same person. This functional approach typically yields two to three times the true code required for a warehouse management system. The more code, the more difficult the system is to maintain and the less reliable it becomes. Instead, by recognizing that all the major functions in the warehouse are derived from combinations of batching, slotting, and sequencing applied to customer and/or purchase orders, new object-oriented warehouse management systems have a much smaller core code. As a result, they are easier to maintain and are more reliable.

This functional approach typically yields two to three times the true code required for a warehouse management system.

4.5
INTELLIGENT SLOTTING

In *slotting,* we determine for each item its:

1. appropriate storage mode,

2. appropriate allocation of space in its appropriate storage mode, and

3. appropriate storage location in its appropriate storage mode.

As a result, slotting has a significant impact on all of the warehouse key performance indicators (WKPIs) - productivity, shipping accuracy, inventory accuracy, dock-to-stock time, warehouse order cycle time, storage density, and the level of automation. Hence, few decisions do more to determine the overall performance of a warehouse than slotting. Nonetheless, very few warehouse management systems and very few warehouses have the data, let alone the engineering and computer support to intelligently slot the warehouse and to keep the slotting aligned with the current warehouse activity profile. Consequently, most warehouses are spending 10% to 30% more per year than they should because the warehouse is improperly slotted.

There are many reasons why most warehouses are improperly slotted - the data is not available, the MIS resources are not available, there is no way to keep the slotting current, there is no methodology for slotting, etc. Here we will try to eliminate these excuses by presenting a methodology that is implemented on a personal computer (*Warehouse Toolbox [9]*) attached to a host or stand-alone warehouse management system that recommends the appropriate slotting for a warehouse on an on-going basis. The ten-step methodology is outlined below.

Most warehouses are spending 10% to 30% more per year than they should because the warehouse is i. properly slotted.

This intelligent slotting methodology is based on many years of research in slotting and recent slotting projects with Adolph Coors, Amoco, Allied Signal, Arrow Electronics, Baptist Sunday School Board, Cardone Industries, Coats & Clark, DuPont, Mack Trucks, Nashua, Northern Telecom, PepsiCo, Polygram, Spartan Stores and Stihl Corporation. After looking back on all those projects and all those different types of items - cans, bottles, and kegs of beer; rolls of carpet backing; brake parts; spools of yarn; computer hardware and software; vials of nuclear medicine; automotive service parts; paper products; telecommunications equipment and parts; frozen food; cassettes and compact disks; perishable food items; and chainsaws - I identified the common denominators of the projects, and developed this ten-step slotting methodology and supporting PC-tool to assist in slotting projects in nearly any industry. An outline of the ten-step slotting methodology and example output from the *Warehouse Toolbox* follows.

CONDUCT A WAREHOUSE OPERATIONS AUDIT

The warehouse operations audit includes a warehouse performance and warehouse practices gap analysis (Chapter 3). The purpose of the audit is to reveal if and how slotting could improve the operations of the warehouse. There are some warehouse operations where because of poor management, poor worker morale, an undisciplined workforce, union-management tensions, poor housekeeping, inadequate computer training and support, and/or a variety of other reasons, intelligent slotting will not improve the performance of the operation. In those cases it does not make sense to carry on with a slotting project.

POPULATE THE SLOTTING DATABASE

Slotting is data intensive. Without comprehensive and accurate data describing the activity, dimensions, and storage characteristics of the items in the warehouse, intelligent slotting is impossible. Fortunately, the number of data elements required for slotting is not overwhelming. An example list of data requirements follows. For each item we need the:

- item number,
- item description,
- material type,
- storage environment (i.e. frozen, refrigerated, flammable, hazardous, etc.),
- shelf life,
- dimensions (L, W, H),
- item unit cube,
- weight,
- units per carton,
- cartons per pallet, and
- base unit of measure.

This information should be readily available from the product or item master file. Just the process of evaluating the accuracy and availability of this data is helpful as a data integrity audit.

For each customer order we need the:

- customer identification,
- unique items requested on the order and the quantities of each, and
- order date and time.

This information should be available from the sales and/or order history file. The sample size required depends heavily on the seasonality of the industry. If there are large annual surges of demand, such as in the mail order and retailing industries, then a 12-month sample is necessary. If the demand is fairly stable over the course of a year, as in automotive service parts, then a three-to six-month sample will be appropriate.

COMPUTE SLOTTING STATISTICS

Once the raw data is captured, the computation of the slotting statistics is fairly straightforward. Unfortunately, the natural interpretation and application of the results may be counter-intuitive and misleading. The family of slotting statistics computable from the slotting database follows.

These statistics appear on the surface to be self-explanatory. However, there are some subtle but critical issues surrounding the interpretation of each statistic. For example, popularity is often incorrectly measured in dollar sales or unit sales. The popularity (P) of an item, like the popularity of a song on a juke box, should be measured by the number of times it is requested. This indicator is critical since it is a measure of the number of potential times an operator will visit the location for a particular item. Since most of the work in a warehouse is traveling to, from, and between warehouse locations, knowledge of the potential location visits for individual and families of items is critical to success in managing the overall work content in the warehouse.

Since most of the work in a warehouse is traveling to, from, and between warehouse locations, knowledge of the potential location visits for individual and families of items is critical to success in managing the overall work content in the warehouse.

Unfortunately, many warehouse managers and analysts stop with popularity in their search for slotting criteria. Popu-

Slotting Statistic	Symbol	Unit(s) of Measure	Notes and Comments
Slotting Period	R	Time (Year, Quarter, Month, week, Day)	The time period for slotting calculations
Popularity	P	Requests per Period	Sometimes referred to as the hits on an item. Used with volume to determine assignment to a storage mode and location within the storage mode.
Turnover	T	Units Shipped per Period	Sometimes referred to as the demand for an item. Used with unit cube to compute cube movement for storage mode assignment and space allocation.
Unit Cube	C	Ft³/unit	Measures the physical size of one unit of a unique item. The information may already be in a database. If not, C can be computed by measuring the size of the outer container for the item (pallet, case, tote, bag, etc.) and dividing by the number of units in the container.
Cube Movement	$V=$ $T \times C$	Ft³/Period	Sometimes referred to as the volume. Used to determine the appropriate storage mode and the allocation of space in the storage mode.
Pick Density	$D=$ P/V	Requests/Ft³	Used in golden zoning. The items with the highest pick density should be assigned to the most accessible picking locations.
Demand Increment	$I=$ T/P	Units per Request	
Standard Deviation of Demand	S		Measure of the daily standard deviation of demand.

Table 4.2 Slotting Statistics, Symbols, and Units of Measure.

larity is used singly to assign items to storage modes, to allocate space in storage modes, and to locate items within storage modes. Let's consider the example of golden zoning a section of bin shelving. The objective is to maximize the amount of picking activity that is done at or near waist level. Assume there is 7 cubic feet of space available in the golden zone. Suppose there are three items we are considering for slotting. The slotting statistics for the three items are recorded in Table 4.3 below.

Item ID	Popularity	Cube-Movement	Pick Dessity
A	140 requests/month	7 ft³/month	20 requests/ft³
B	108 requests/month	4 ft³/month	27 requests/ft³
C	75 requests/month	3 ft³/month	25 requests/ft³

Table 4.3 Slotting Example.

Suppose we decide to store a month's supply of material in bin shelving. Item A requires 7 cubic feet, item B requires 4 cubic feet, and item C requires 3 cubic feet. Suppose we rank the items based on popularity alone to determine the order of preference for assignment into the golden zone. (Remember the golden zone only has 7 cubic feet of capacity). With the popularity ranking, item A will be assigned to (and will exhaust the available space in) the golden zone. There will be 140 visits to the golden zone per month. (Remember we are trying to maximize the number of trips to the golden zone.) Is that the best we can do? Absolutely not! Suppose we assign items B and C to the golden zone. In/that case, there will be 183 trips to the golden zone. Had we used pick density as the criteria for the preference ranking, we would have maximized the activity in the golden zone. That is why that measure of picking activity is so critical to the success of slotting, and consequently why it is so important to have all of the slotting statistics available.

CONSTRUCT THE WAREHOUSE ACTIVITY PROFILE

The slotting statistics and order files should be used to develop a full warehouse activity profile. The composition of a warehouse activity profile was fully explained in Chapter 2. With those profiles in hand, the next step is to define item families for family slotting. Two profiles that were not explained in Chapter 2 that are critical for slotting are the picking mode profile and the operations planning profile. The picking mode profile defines the picking modes that are being considered. An example picking mode profile for broken case picking systems is presented in Table 4.4.

	Bin Shelving	Flow Rack	Storage Drawers	Horizontal Carousels	Vertical Carousels	Miniload ASRS	Automated Dispensing
Retrieval Method	n/a	n/a	n/a	n/a	n/a	n/a	n/a
Communication Method	n/a	n/a	n/a	n/a	n/a	n/a	n/a
Pick Rate (Lines per person-Hour)	90	70	50	150	80	60	1200
Restocking Rate (Restocks per Person-Hour)	45	60	30	40	35	35	400
Time Supply (Days)	20	5	20	10	20	20	20
Picking Accuracy	0,95	0.95	0.95	0.95	0.95	0.95	0.95
Net Investment Cost ($/CF)	$15.00	$30.00	$40.00	$50.00	$75.00	$65.00	$300.00
PTL Display Cost per SKU	$200.00	$200.00	$120.00	$40.00	$60.00	n/a	n/a
Footprint Density (CF/SF)	1.17	0.5	2	12	6	4	12

Table 4.4. Example Picking Mode Profile (CF=cubic feet, SF=square feet).

An operations planning profile defines the design and economic analysis parameters upon which operations design decisions, including slotting, will be based. An example operations planning profile is presented in Table 4.5.

Planning Criteria	Value	Unit of Measure
Wage Rate	$11.00	$ per Hour
Occupancy Cost	$5.00	$ per Square Foot per Year
Planning Horizon	5	Years
Working Days per Year	250	Days
Working Hours per Day	12	Hours per Day
Error Cost	$30.00	$ per Error

Table 4.5. Example Operations Planning Profile.

ASSIGN ITEMS TO ITEM FAMILIES

Guided by the warehouse activity profiles, the next step is to assign items to item families. The process is a progressive sifting process. The steps of the sifting process are outlined below.

i.) Assign items to *storage environment families* based on requirements for storage temperature (frozen, refrigerated, and ambient), flammability, and/or hazardous storage. These storage environment families will specify the need for special building requirements, special racking requirements, and special material handling zones.

ii.) Within each storage environment, assign items to *order completion zones* based on the order completion and demand correlation analysis completed in warehouse activity profiling. These order completion zones will create warehouses within the warehouse for highly efficient order picking.

iii.) Within each storage environment, within each order completion zone, assign items to *item activity families* based on cube movement, popularity, and pick density families. These families will be the basis for assigning items to storage modes, allocating space within storage modes, and assigning specific locations within the storage modes.

ASSIGN ITEM ACTIVITY FAMILIES TO STORAGE MODE FAMILIES

Based on productivity, storage density, picking error rates, and system investment requirements, a storage mode economic analysis should determine the least cost storage mode for each item. The items assigned to a particular storage mode become the members of that storage mode's family. The *Warehouse Toolbox* slotting module computes the annualized cost of assigning each item to each storage mode. The least cost mode is recommended for each item. Example output from the *Warehouse Toolbox* illustrates (Figure 4.7) the assignment of item activity families to storage mode families.

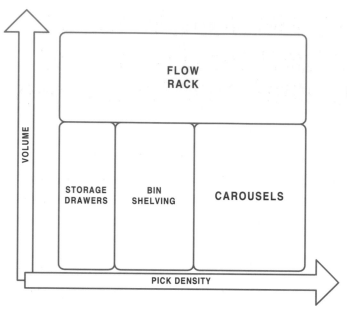

Figure 4.7a. Example Item Activity Family to Storage Mode Family
Analysis for Broken Case Picking.

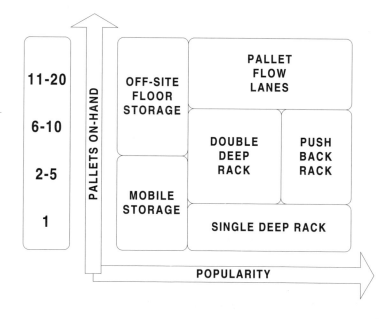

Figure 4.7b. Example Item Activity Family to Storage Mode Family
Analysis for Pallet Storage and Retrieval.

Map the Individual Warehouse Locations within Each Storage Mode into Picking Activity Zones

The first step in this mapping is to plot the pick path through each storage mode. Once the pick path through the pick line has been determined, the definition of the activity zones is fairly straightforward.

The two most popular pick paths are the serpentine pick path and the mainline path with side trips (see Figure 4.8).

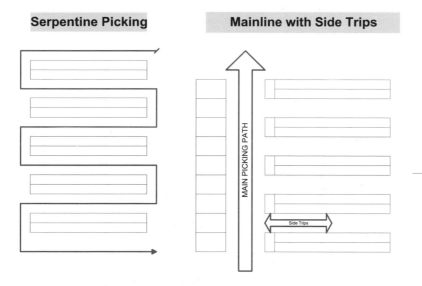

Figure 4.8 Serpentine Picking and Mainline Picking with Side Trips.

In *serpentine picking*, the order picker will by definition travel down each aisle and by each location. Hence, to designate an A activity zone near one end of the pick line will not reduce travel time. In fact, it may create congestion problems.

Instead, the A activity zone should be defined as the locations that are at or near waist level for broken case picking, and at or near floor-level for case picking from pallet rack.

In *mainline picking with side trips*, the objective is to minimize the number and length of the side trips. Hence, the A activity zone should be defined as the locations along the mainline.

In order picking from a pod of two or three carousels, picking from alternating carousels should eliminate any idle time for the order picker waiting on the carousel, and the A activity zone should be defined as the locations at or near waist level.

An example mapping of storage mode locations into activity zones is illustrated in Figure 4.9.

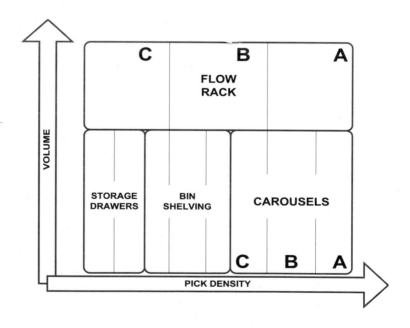

Figure 4.9. Example Mapping of Storage Mode Locations into Activity Zones.

Assign Items to Storage Mode Activity Zones Based on Pick Density

Beginning with the item with the highest pick density (and in descending order of pick density), begin assigning items to the A activity zone, then the B zone, and finally the C zone until the list of items is exhausted. An example assignment of items to storage modes and pick zones is illustrated in Table 4.6.

Table 4.6. Example Slotting Assignment Output [Warehouse Toolbox].

Item ID	Mode	Zone	Pick Face
013710	Horizontal Carousels	A	0.929
307015	Horizontal Carousels	A	4.258
306001	Horizontal Carousels	A	4.323
307014	Horizontal Carousels	A	20.457
018015	Horizontal Carousels	B	0.692
322002	Horizontal Carousels	B	1.213
245009	Horizontal Carousels	B	1.243
328002	Horizontal Carousels	B	1.915
322001	Horizontal Carousels	B	2.883
244318	Horizontal Carousels	C	0.461
322004	Horizontal Carousels	C	0.609
375893	Horizontal Carousels	C	0.878
307008	Horizontal Carousels	C	0.924
323004	Horizontal Carousels	C	1.878
319706	Horizontal Carousels	C	2.446
326006	Horizontal Carousels	C	3.506
307016	Flow Rack	A	7.166
307002	Flow Rack	A	8.008
081093	Flow Rack	A	9.780
322008	Flow Rack	A	9.899
307012	Flow Rack	A	10.061
318001	Flow Rack	A	10.828
245574	Flow Rack	A	11.211
315002	Flow Rack	A	11.448
011390	Flow Rack	A	11.762
307013	Flow Rack	A	11.951
330001	Flow Rack	A	12.473
317001	Flow Rack	A	70.468
015103	Flow Rack	A	79.992
015409	Flow Rack	A	82.628

Specify Reslotting Rules

Unfortunately, almost as soon as an item is properly slotted, its activity profile changes. For example, in the mail order industry changes in catalogs yield major changes to the warehouse activity profile and major changes to the slotting requirements. Hence, it is critical to maintain a current slotting to maintain the productivity and storage density gains that are achieved under the initial slotting program.

Based on the initial slotting, reslotting rules should be defined to suggest when and if a particular item should be reslotted. The rules can be developed with the help of a simple from-to chart which computes the potential cost savings of moving an item from its current mode and zone to every other mode and zone. This savings is compared with the cost to move the item. If the savings-to-cost ratio exceeds a predetermined threshold, the item is recommended for reslotting. Note that a more convenient opportunity for reslotting an item occurs when its pick location inventory drops to zero. In that case, the slotting system should suggest the most appropriate slotting for the item and direct the restocking operator to the new location for the item.

Perhaps a more difficult question is the timing of a general reslotting of the entire warehouse. Unfortunately, there is very little science to go on here. Most warehouses have a natural demand rhythm. For example, L.L. Bean, the mail order catalog operator, drops four main catalogs a year - Winter, Spring, Fall, and Summer. It is natural in that case to reslot the warehouse every season. In some operations there is a slow period at the first of the year. That may be a perfect time to reslot the warehouse. Avon Products has 26 promotional campaigns a year. The warehouse has to be reslotted 26 times a year.

BAPTIST SUNDAY SCHOOL BOARD

The Baptist Sunday School Board publishes and distributes Christian media (books, periodicals, cassette tapes, compact disks, videos, etc.) and gift items to bookstores (retail distribution), churches (church distribution), and individuals (mail order) all over the United States. More than 15,000 items are housed in its 600,000 square foot distribution center in downtown Nashville, Tennessee. The reserve inventory for each business unit is centralized and housed in high-bay, random locations. The forward, picking inventory is housed in dedicated locations on separate low-bay picking floors for each business unit. Since the business is a low-margin business, there is little or no capital available for highly mechanized systems. Hence, the design strategy is to eliminate and streamline as much work content as possible.

The slotting and layout plan for the retail picking floor is illustrated in Figure 4.10. Note the main, horseshoe pick line in the center of the warehouse. While traversing this pick line, order pickers pick approximately 20 orders per pass. A specially designed cart organized to hold 24 orders allows the pickers to quickly and efficiently sort individual picks into orders as they go. Items with the highest cube-movement are housed in carton flow racks in the center of the layout. Since each picking tour will pass each flow rack bay, the picking activity is purposefully distributed evenly along

This slotting scheme alleviates any congestion problems and allows nearly 75% of the picks to be executed along the main pick line.

the flow rack pick line. The most popular flow rack items are located in the golden zone for the flow rack, the level of the flow rack a⁺ or near waist level. The remainder of the items fall naturally into bin shelving. To minimize travel time, the bin shelving items with the greatest pick density are assigned to the locations along or near the pick line. This slotting scheme alleviates any congestion problems and allows nearly 75% of the picks to be executed along the main pick line. The reserve stock for the gravity flow lanes is housed in double-deep pallet rack along the back wall. Batched replenishments are executed along the back of the flow lanes. Reserve stock for the bin shelving is conveniently located in single-deep pallet rack along the side walls.

This slotting and operating scheme yielded a 100% improvement in productivity and response time with minimal capital investment and rist.

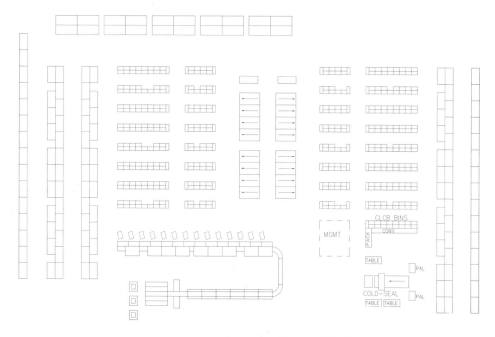

Figure 4.10 Example Slotting Plan and Warehouse Layout.

4.6
INTELLIGENT BATCHING

Intelligent batching schemes group picks, putaways, and replenishments into efficient worksets. Examples of good batching practice are batching single line orders for special picking tours and batching a pick and putaway that are in nearby locations for interleaving. Since the most opportunity in batching is in the area of order picking, the remainder of this section is devoted to batching for order picking.

The good news on batching for order picking is that there are only four basic batching schemes:

- *single order picking* in which an order picker picks a single order at a time,

- *batch picking* in which an order picker picks multiple orders in a picking tour, sorting the picks into orders as he goes,

- *progressive assembly* of an order by passing its contents from zone to zone, and

- *wave picking*.

The trick is to select the proper approach for your warehouse and if we are sophisticated enough, to marry different order types to different batching strategies in the same warehouse. To assist warehouse operators with batching decision I developed an order picking policy decision tree. The decision tree is presented in Figure 4.11 below.

Marry different order types to different batching strategies in the same warehouse.

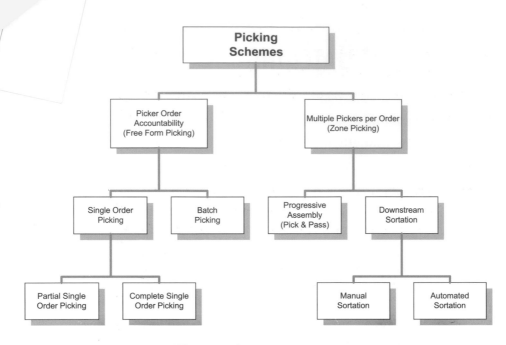

Figure 4.11 Order Picking Policy Desision Tree.

The first decision is whether or not to organize order picking by assigning operators to picking/putaway zones. A picking zone is defined as a portion of an aisle, multiple aisles, or machines (carousels, ASRS machines) assigned to an operator for picking and/or putaway. The key distinguishing feature is that the operator is dedicated to a zone and no other operator works in that zone. In order picking this also means that the operators do not have order completion accountability since the lines on an order will be filled from different zones and hence by different order pickers. (A storage zone is distinguished from a picking zone. Storage zones are defined to facilitate efficient and safe storage. For example, storage zones may be established for bulky items, floor storage items, small items, bar stock items, refrigerated items, frozen items, flammable items, explosive items, etc. These zones are specified in slotting.)

The opposite of zoning for order picking is free-form picking. In free-form picking, order pickers are responsible for picking every line on each order assigned to them and they are free to move to any aisle in the warehouse. The pros and cons of creating picking zones are highlighted in Table 4.7 below.

Zoning Pros	Notes and Comments
Operator travel time is reduced since operators are assigned to small, dedicated work areas.	I always prefer to play zone defense in basketball since I do not have to chase anyone around the court and since I do not have responsibility for an opposing player's scoring outbursts!
Operators become familiar with the products and locations in their zone.	Product famililiarity should yield improved picking productivity and picking accuracy. (See Xerox Service parts below.)
Congestion is minimized since not more than one operator is in an aisle at a time.	Minimizing congestion is the most important justification for zone picking. In some operations the volume is so great that free-form picking creates grid-lock like bottlenecks.
There is operator-zone accountability.	The order picking performance (productivity, accuracy, housekeeping) can be recorded and posted by zone. The tradeoff is the loss in accountability for orders. (See True Value Hardware below.)
Minimizes excessive socializing.	Since operators are assigned alone to dedicated work zones, there is little or no opportunity during a pick wave for excessive socializing. Some socializing is healthy, but zone picking helps to control and monitor it.

Table 4.7 To Zone or Not to Zone?

Xerox Service Parts

I recently toured a Xerox service parts distribution center outside of Chicago, Illinois. During the tour I spent nearly an hour observing the order picking operation. In that operation, order pickers are each assigned to a zone of two long aisles of bin shelving. Orders are progressively assembled by conveying an order tote from zone to zone.

I especially enjoyed meeting the top performing order picker. She had been with Xerox for over 20 years and had worked the same two aisles in the warehouse for over three years. The housekeeping, productivity, and accuracy in her zone were the highest in the warehouse. Her pride in her job was also evident by the near-perfect arrangement of the merchandise in her zone. I could not help but comment to her about the excellent performance record she had and on the neatness of her work area. During the conversation I noticed that the merchandise in the bin closest to the front of her zone and next to the takeaway conveyor was not nearly as neatly arranged as the other bins. It was so unusual compared to other bins in her zone that we asked her about the arrangement of that particular bin. She told me the bin contained merchandise that customers were going to order that day. How did she know that? She did not have ESP or claim to function as the world's greatest forecasting system. The items in that bin were A-movers that had not been properly reslotted. The order picker grew tired of traveling to the end of her zone for those popular items. She simply moved some of the inventory for those items close to the front of the zone. This simple process improvement would have been impossible without the product and location familiarity that comes with zone picking.

COTTER & COMPANY - TRUE VALUE HARDWARE

Cotter & Company is the logistics subsidiary of True Value Hardware. Each of its small item order picking areas is configured in single-aisle zones. A takeaway belt conveyor runs down the center of each zone, allowing an operator to make one pass through the zone during a pick wave. During a pass, each operator works with a roll of picking labels. The labels present items in location sequence to the order picker who picks an item, places a bar code label on the item, places the labeled item on the belt conveyor and moves to the next location. The takeaway belt conveyor feeds a downstream sortation system which sorts the items coming from each zone into retail store orders. At the end of each zone, the performance statistics including picking productivity, picking accuracy (via internal audit), and housekeeping for the zone are posted. Talk about public accountability!

The benefits of zone picking - reduced travel time, minimal congestion, product-location familiarity, and operator-zone accountability - may or may not pay for the associated costs and inherent control complexities presented by zone picking. Table 4.8 below describes some of those costs and control difficulties.

In deciding whether or not zone picking makes sense, I recommend a formal economic and feasibility evaluation of the two picking policies - zone vs. free-form picking. The analysis should compare the best free-form picking design with a zone picking scheme. Zone picking will be the right answer if there are enough incremental benefits (productivity and

The benefits of zone picking - reduced travel time, minimal congestion, product-location familiarity, and operator-zone accountability - may or may not pay for the associated costs and inherent control complexities presented by zone picking.

minimized congestion) to pay for the additional investment cost of the zone picking system. I encourage you to try to devise free-form picking schemes that are so productive that it becomes nearly impossible to justify the additional investments in material and information handling systems required by zone picking. If the zone picking scheme is justifiable when compared to a highly efficient free-form scheme, then you can be confident that the justification is correct. Another approach is to try to configure a zone picking scheme that does not require a major investment in material and information handling systems. An example of this approach is in place at Lanier Worldwide.

Zone Picking Costs and Control Challenges	Notes and Comments
Order assembly.	The major difficulty and cost factor in zone picking is the need to assemble the order across order picking zones. The two methods for order assembly, progressive assembly by passing the contents of the order from zone-to-zone, and wave picking with downtream sortation, can be excessively expensive. They can also reduce the operating flexibility of the warehouse, and significantly increase the level of sophistication of warehouse control systems.
Workload imbalances can create bottlenecks, gridlock, and low worker morale.	It is nearly impossible to perfectly balance the workload between zones on a daily basis. To do so requires advanced soltting techniques or as is the case with highly sophisticated zone schemes, dynamic floating zones are used. In those operations the size of the zone varies as a function of the associated workload. In either case, the controls are an order of magnitude more complex than those used in free-form picking.

Table 4.8 Zone Picking Costs and Control Complexities.

LANIER WORLDWIDE

Lanier Worldwide is a $1 billion distributor of copiers, fax machines, and dictation equipment. A major portion of its revenue comes from service parts and supplies that support its installation base. For parts and supplies picking, Lanier has devised a manual wave-zone picking concept. Parts and supplies are stored in traditional bin shelving. Operators are assigned to zones of 4 aisles of shelving (see Figure 4.12). Orders are released to the picking floor in 20 minute waves, just long enough to allow efficient picking tours and just short enough to maintain the attention and sense of urgency of the order pickers. Each order picker takes a specially designed picking cart through his/her zone. Each picking cart is sub-divided into eight compartments. Before each picking tour, an empty tote labeled with that zone and operator's identification is placed in each of the eight containers. At the beginning of each wave, an order picker is given a pick list which walks the operator through his/her zone in location sequence. On each line on the pick list is the location, the item identification, the quantity to pick, and the number of the compartment (1-8) on the cart to place the item into. At the end of a tour, each order picker brings his/her cart to a large storage rack that is subdivided into (you guessed it) eight compartments. Each operator puts his/her #1 tote in the #1 compartment, his/her #2 tote in the #2 compartment, ... Standing on the other side of the storage compartment is an operator whose job it is to sort the merchandise in each compartment into orders, check the order for accuracy, and pack the contents of the order for shipping. This operation yields manual picking productivity in excess of 120 lines per person-hour and exceptionally high picking accuracy.

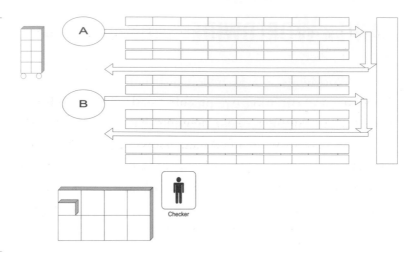

Figure 4.12 Lanier Manual Wave Picking Concept.

As we begin to conceptualize picking schemes for zone picking and free-form picking, the number of alternative schemes within each policy is limited. In free-form picking an order picker is assigned to pick one order at a time during his/her picking tour. This policy is called *single order picking*. The other free-form picking method is *batch picking*. In batch picking each order picker is assigned multiple orders to pick at a time during his/her picking tour - the order pickers sorting picks into individual orders as they go.

A Trip to the Grocery Store

Let's consider the pros and cons of single order and batch picking. You can make the comparison by thinking about a trip to the grocery store. Suppose you take your list of 10 items to the grocery store. Since you don't know the layout of the store, you have to walk down each aisle to make sure you don't miss anything and have to backtrack. To walk each aisle of the store requires that you walk 1,000 feet - 100 feet per item picked.

Now suppose you call your neighbor and offer to do his or her grocery shopping. Your neighbor has 10 items as well. You still have to walk 1,000 feet. However, this time you pick 20 items - 50 feet per pick - as opposed to just 10 items - 100 feet per pick. The benefits are obvious. The savings in travel time should more than offset the work in keeping the contents of the orders separated.

Now suppose you get carried away with all these benefits of batch picking, and you call everyone in the neighborhood and offer to do their grocery shopping for them. This time you have 1,000 items to select in walking the same 1,000 feet. You only walk 1 foot per line item. However, the work required to keep the merchandise separated and the mega-cart that is required to contain the merchandise makes this an impossible task.

The example illustrates the major benefit of batch picking vs. single order picking - less travel time per item picked. The tendency then is to add as many orders to a picking tour as possible. That is indeed the objective; however, there is a point where the physical capacity of the picking vehicle and/or the mental capacity of the order picker constrains the number of orders in the picking tour. In general though, we would like to add as many orders to the tour as the order picker can physically and mentally manage.

With this obvious benefit of batch picking vs. single order picking, when would you ever choose to pick just one order at a time? First, some orders are large enough (number of picks or cubic volume) to make an efficient picking tour unto themselves. Second, as the number of orders in a tour increases, the likelihood of a picking/sorting error increases. Some companies are so accuracy conscious that they will only allow an order picker to select a single order at a time. Third, to pick more than one order at a time means there must be more than one order to pick. This may mean waiting for orders to accumulate to allow efficient picking tours. For an emergency order, the customer service motivation should override the efficiency motivation, and we should pick the single emergency order.

The two zone picking operating policies are *progressive order assembly* (POA) and *wave picking with downstream sortation*. In progressive order assembly (see Figure 4.13), the contents of an order are passed from one zone to the next until the order is completely assembled. The contents of the order may move in a tote pan or carton on a conveyor from zone to zone, may be manually moved on a cart from zone to zone, or may move on pallets on a towline conveyor, automated guided vehicle, lift truck or pallet jack from zone to zone. Intelligent POA systems will only move an order's container to a zone if there is an SKU for the order in that particular zone. This practice is called *zone skipping*.

In wave picking with downstream sortation (see Figure 4.14), there is no designation of an order during the picking process. Order pickers work in parallel making full passes of their pick zone during a wave. Product is typically bar code labeled as it is picked and placed into a large cart or onto a conveyor belt that passes alongside the pick line. The contents of the cart and/or the items on the takeaway conveyor are then inducted into a sortation system which sorts the

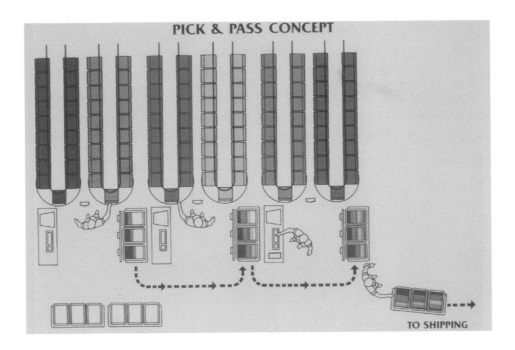

PICK & PASS CONCEPT

TO SHIPPING

Figure 4.13 Progressive Order Assembly with Carousels [White].

merchandise into customer orders. The cost of downstream sortation systems can run into the millions of dollars. Hence, the incremental benefits of wave picking with downstream sortation compared to progressive order assembly must be sufficient to justify the incremental investment. The incremental benefits are primarily picking productivity benefits. The incremental cost is the difference between the cost of the material and information handling systems required for downstream sorting vs. that required for passing the order contents from zone to zone.

To decide from among these four picking policies I recommend that a concept be developed based on each of the four picking paradigms. Beginning with single order picking and moving to batch picking, then to progressive order assembly, then to wave picking with downstream sortation, an incremental justification of the concepts should be conducted. From that justification process, a policy should be selected and implemented. Whatever the justified policy, the flexibility to single order pick and batch pick based on the characteristics of certain orders should be designed into the system.

The flexibility to single order pick and batch pick based on the characteristics of certain orders should be designed into the system.

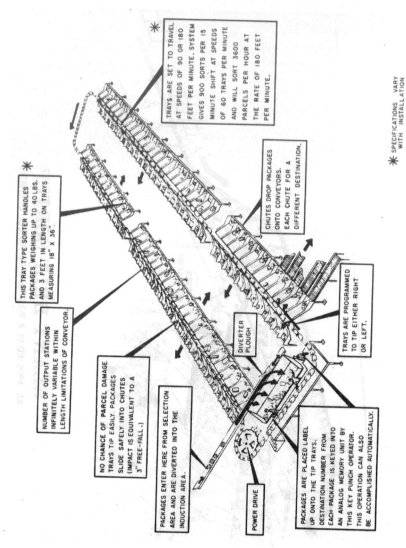

Figure 4.14a. Tilt-tray Sorting System for Downstream Sortation [25].

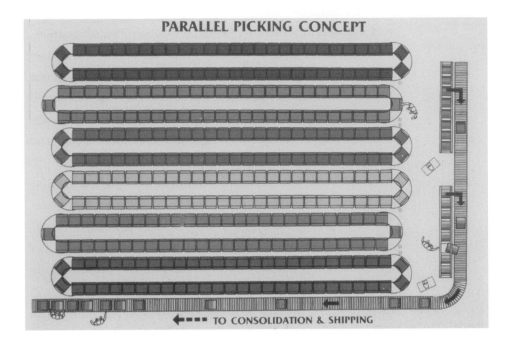

PARALLEL PICKING CONCEPT

◄■■■ TO CONSOLIDATION & SHIPPING

Figure 4.14b. Typical Wave Picking Configuration for Carousels [White].

4.7

INTELLIGENT SEQUENCING

Intelligent sequencing is the practice of sequencing picking, putaway, and restocking transactions in a manner that minimizes travel time and maximizes operator productivity. After the complexities of intelligent slotting and batching, transaction sequencing is often taken for granted in warehouse operations. Unfortunately, improper sequencing can undo all the productivity gains that should have been realized via intelligent slotting and batching. The key to proper sequencing is to design minimum distance picking, putaway, restocking, and interleaving tours of the warehouse locations. In the simplest case of picking along or restocking a fixed picking line, the operator should simply be directed in location sequence along the line. In the more complex cases of picking, putaway, and restocking tours from scattered warehouse locations, the sequencing algorithm should construct minimum-distance travel tours. In addition, opportunities for interleaving picks, putaways, and restocking transactions into the same tour should be leveraged. An even more complex sequencing challenge occurs in case picking to a pallet, where the objectives are first to build a stable pallet load that does not crush lightweight items on the bottom of the pallet, and second to minimize travel time. In this scenario, the sequencing should be facilitated by assigning the large, heavy items at the front of the pick line with the items becoming smaller and lighter as the picker proceeds along the pick line. (Kodak recently built an expert system to rationalize these competing sequencing objectives - pallet stability, zero crushing, and minimal travel time - and to design optimal picking tours.)

4.8
SUMMARY

1. *Direct shipping and cross-docking.* Maximize and plan for direct shipping and cross-docking for all those items and orders where direct shipping and cross-docking are feasible and justifiable.

2. *Pre-packaging.* Pre-package in increments that customers are likely to order in and encourage customers to order in full handling unit increments.

3. *Pick from storage.* When feasible and justifiable, pick broken case and full case quantities directly from reserve storage locations.

4. *Work simplification.* Eliminate and combine order picking tasks to streamline work content.

5. *Intelligent slotting.* Use key item slotting attributes including storage environment requirements, popularity, cube movement, and demand correlation to assign each item to its appropriate location and allocation of space in its appropriate storage mode.

   . Conduct a warehouse operations audit.

   . Populate the slotting database.

   . Compute slotting statistics.

   . Construct the warehouse activity profile.

   . Assign items to item families.

   . Assign item activity families to storage mode families.

   . Map the individual warehouse locations within each storage mode into picking activity zones.

. Based on pick density, assign items to storage mode activity zones.

. Specify reslotting rules.

6. ***Intelligent batching.*** Batch orders, putaways, and replenishments into efficient worksets.

7. ***Intelligent sequencing.*** Sequence picking, putaway, and restocking transactions to minimize travel time and maximize operator productivity.

COMPUTERIZING
WAREHOUSE OPERATIONS

The proper role for the computer in warehouse operations is to help warehouse managers manage and to help warehouse operators operate. For managers, the computer should:

- continuously profile warehouse activity to help managers pinpoint and anticipate problem areas and major shifts in activity levels and patterns;

- continuously monitor warehouse performance in productivity, shipping and inventory accuracy, warehouse order cycle time, and storage density; and

- continuously simplify the warehouse operations by reliably communicating transactions to/from warehouse operators and equipment.

For warehouse operators, the WMS should facilitate hands-free and paperless activities. It is that simple. If the WMS does not help the warehouse manager manage and the warehouse operators operate, what good is it? With over 400 providers of warehouse management systems aggressively marketing their products and in-house MIS groups eagerly encouraging system improvements, it is easy to lose sight of the fundamental improvements that computerizing warehouse operations should bring.

> *If the WMS does not help the warehouse manager manage and the warehouse operators operate, what good is it?*

This chapter is not meant to be an exhaustive description of warehouse management system functions, features, strategies, and supplier alternatives. That's a book, not a chapter. In addition, warehouse management systems are not my area of expertise. Leveraging the capabilities of warehouse management systems, however, is my expertise and it is critical to achieving world-class warehousing. In fact, I believe it is so critical to success in warehousing that the sequel to this book is already in the works and it is titled, *Computer-Aided Warehousing*.

Since the focus of this book is operational excellence, I have targeted two aspects of computerized warehousing that can make or break the operations. The first section of the chapter is a review of paperless warehousing devices and systems. Paperless warehousing devices are the interface between the warehouse operators and the warehouse management system. Hence, the design and selection of these devices and systems is critical to the success of the overall operation. The second section of the chapter is a collection of recommendations on selecting, justifying and implementing warehouse management systems. I have witnessed this process take a warehouse ahead ten years and set it behind by ten years.

Information Technology for Paperless Warehousing

A full information technology solution for warehouse operations includes:

- a computing platform (i.e. mainframe, mid-range, client-server network, and/or network of personal computers),

- a network of paperless devices (i.e.radio frequency terminals, bar code scanners, light-directed systems, voice headsets),

- a relational and/or object database (i.e. Oracle, Sybase, Informix, and/or proprietary),

- warehouse management software,

- enterprise system interface software, and

- material handling and paperless device interface software.

Since there is already extensive material published on computing platforms, relational and object-oriented databases, and warehouse management software, this chapter focuses on paperless warehousing systems. Please see [10] for a review of computing platform alternatives, [11] for a description of relational and/or object-oriented databases, and [12] for a review of warehouse management software alternatives. Software for interfacing with enterprise systems, material handling devices, and paperless warehousing systems is typically proprietary in nature.

Each year The Logistics Institute at Georgia Tech conducts a survey to determine industry priorities for warehouse management systems functionality [6]. Last year the top three priorities were (1) paperless communications, (2) live inventory, and (3) productivity tracking.

Why is "paperless" the top priority? Many of the potholes on the road to world-class warehousing are related to paper and paper handling. First, it is easy to lose paper. I do it every day. Second, you have to read paper. Reading warehouse documents usually requires searching through a maze of information for just a single line that matters for the transaction at hand. As a result, transpositions can occur. Third, you have to write on paper. Again, it is easy to transpose something. Fourth, things on paper cannot be communicated in real time. As a result, errors in inventory levels and/or order status are never known. It is difficult to do cross-docking and transaction interleaving. Fifth, paper is expensive to print, handle, and file. Sixth, it is easy to damage and smudge paper. Paperless warehousing and world-class warehousing go hand in hand!

Many warehousing professionals automatically link paperless warehousing with bar coding and radio frequency data communication. While those technologies do indeed support paperless warehousing, there is a proliferating list of new paperless warehousing technologies, some of which may be much more appropriate for your application than bar coding and RF data communications. The two system components required for paperless warehousing are automatic identification media and paperless communication systems. Automatic identification media is required to al-

Many of the potholes on the road to world-class warehousing are related to paper and paper handling.

WORLD-CLASS WAREHOUSING © EDWARD H. FRAZELLE PH.D.

low a machine to recognize an object. Paperless communication systems are required to automate the communication and identification of the recognized objects and to transmit system instructions and updates to warehouse operators.

Automatic Identification Media

Automated *status control* of material requires that the real-time awareness of the location, amount, origin, destination, and schedule of material be achieved automatically. This objective is in fact the function of automatic identification technologies; to permit real-time, defect-free data collection. Examples of automatic identification technologies at work include:

- A vision system reading labels to identify the proper destination for a carton traveling on a sortation conveyor.

- A laser scanner relaying the inventory levels of a small parts warehouse to a computer via RF.

- A voice recognition system to identify parts received at the receiving dock.

- A radio frequency (RF) or surface acoustical wave (SAW) tag used to permanently identify a tote pan.

- A card with a magnetic stripe traveling with a unit load to identify the load through the distribution channels.

The automatic identification mediums used to support these transactions include bar codes, optical characters, radio frequency tags, and magnetic stripes on smart cards.

Bar Code Systems

A bar code system includes a bar code *symbology* to represent a series of alphanumeric characters, bar code *readers* to interpret the bar code symbology, and bar code *printers* to reliably and accurately print bar codes on labels, cartons, and/or picking/shipping documents. The review is included here because bar code systems are the foundation of many paperless warehousing systems. The review is meant only as a brief introduction to bar code systems. Please consult [13,14,15] for a full review of bar code systems.

Bar Code Symbologies

A bar code (Figure 5.1) is a series of printed bars and intervening spaces. The structure of unique bar/space patterns represents various alphanumeric characters. The same pattern may represent different alphanumeric characters in different codes.

Figure 5.1 Example Bar Code.

WORLD-CLASS WAREHOUSING © EDWARD H. FRAZELLE PH.D.

The primary codes or symbologies for which standards have been developed include:

- *Code 39*: An alpha-numeric code adopted by a wide number of industry and government organizations for both individual product identification and shipping package/container identification.

- *Interleaved 2 of 5 Code*: A compact, numeric-only code still used in a number of applications where alpha-numeric encoding is not required.

- *Universal Product Code (UPC)*: Used to record the unique product identifier on retail products.

- *Codabar*: One of the earlier symbols developed, this symbol permits encoding of the numeric-character set, six unique control characters and four unique stop/start characters that can be used to distinguish different item classifications. It is primarily used in non-grocery retail point of sale applications, blood banks and libraries.

- *Code 93*: Accommodating all 128 ASCII characters plus 43 alpha-numeric characters and four control characters, Code 93 offers the highest alpha-numeric data density of the six standard symbologies. In addition to allowing for positive switching between ASCII and alpha-numeric, the code uses two check characters to ensure data integrity.

- *Code 128*: Provides the architecture for high density encoding of the full 128 character ASCII set, variable length fields and elaborate character-by-character and full symbol integrity checking. Provides the highest numeric-only data density. Adopted in 1989 by the Uniform Code Council (U.S.) and the International Article Number Association (EAN) for shipping container identification.

- *UPC/EAN*: The numeric-only symbols developed for grocery supermarket point-of-sale applications and now widely used in a variety of other retailing environments. Fixed length code suitable for unique manufacturer and item identification only.

- *Stacked Symbologies*: Although a consensus standard has not yet emerged, the health and electronics industries have initiated programs to evaluate the feasibility of using Code 16K or Code 49, two microsymbologies that offer significant potential for small item encoding. Packing data in from two to sixteen stacked rows, Code 16K accommodates the full 128-character ASCII set and permits the encoding of up to 77 characters in an area of less than .5 square inches. Comparable in terms of data density, Code 49 also handles the full ASCII character set. It encodes data in from two to eight rows and has a capacity of up to 49 alpha-numeric characters per symbol.

- *Two Dimensional Codes*: Two-dimensional bar codes, sometimes referred to as high-density bar codes, are the latest development in a rapidly advancing field. Two-dimensional codes are overlapping linear bar codes, one horizontal and the other vertical in the same field. These codes permit the automatic encoding of nearly a printed page's worth of text in a square inch of page space. Examples include Code 49, Code 16k, PDF 417, Code One, Datamatrix, and UPS's Maxicode.

Bar codes can be and are used in warehousing for:

- product identification,
- container identification,
- location identification,
- operator identification,
- equipment identification, and
- document identification.

The tendency is to get caught up in bar coding for the sake of bar coding, trying to bar code anything and everything in the warehouse. The key to success is to minimize the amount of bar coding required to achieve the automatic communications objectives of the warehouse. If there is too much bar coding and too much bar code scanning, the costs and time to print and scan all the codes can quickly negate potential productivity and accuracy benefits.

The key to success is to minimize the amount of bar coding required to achieve the automatic communications objectives of the warehouse. If there is too much bar coding and too much bar code scanning, the costs and time to print and scan all the codes can quickly negate potential productivity and accuracy benefits.

Bar Code Readers

Bar codes are read by both contact and non-contact scanners. Contact scanners must contact the bar code. They can be portable or stationary and typically come in the form of a wand or a light pen. The wand/pen is manually passed across the bar code. The scanner emits either white or infrared light from the wand/pen tip and reads the light pattern that is reflected from the bar code. This information is stored in solid-state memory for subsequent transmission to a computer.

Contact readers (Figure 5.2) are excellent substitutes for keyboard or manual data entry. Alphanumeric information is processed at a rate of up to 50 inches per minute, and the error rate for a basic scanner connected to its decode is 1 in 1,000,000 reads. Light pen or wand scanners with decoder and interface cost around $2,500.

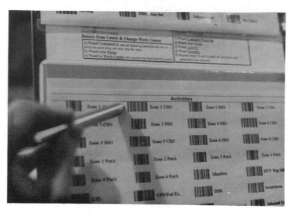

Figure 5.2 Light Pen Scanner.

Non-contact readers (Figure 5.3) may be handheld or stationary and include fixed-beam scanners, moving-beam scanners, and charged couple device (CCD) scanners. Non-contact scanners employ fixed-beam, moving beam, video camera or raster scanning technology to take from one to several hundred looks at the code as it passes. Most bar code scanners read codes bi-directionally by virtue of sophisticated decoding electronics which distinguish the unique start/stop codes peculiar to each symbology and decipher them accordingly. Further, the majority of scanner suppliers now provide equipment with an auto-discrimination feature that permits recognition, reading and verification of multiple symbol formats with no internal or external adjustments. Finally, at least two suppliers have introduced omnidirectional scanners for industrial applications that are capable of reading bar codes passing through a large viewfield at high speeds, regardless of the orientation of the bar code. These scanners are commonly used in high-speed sortation systems.

Figure 5.3 Handheld Laser Scanner.

Fixed-beam readers (Figure 5.4) use a stationary light source to scan a bar code. They depend on the motion of the object to be scanned to move past the beam. Fixed-beam readers rely on consistent, accurate code placement on the moving object.

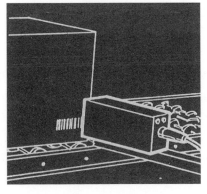

Figure 5.4 Fixed Beam Scanner.

Optical Character Recognition Systems

Optical characters are human and machine readable. The digits at the bottom of a bank check are the most common use of optical characters. Optical character recognition (OCR) systems read alphanumeric data encoded in optical characters so that people as well as computers can interpret the information. An OCR label is read with a hand-held scanner, much like a bar code. OCR systems operate at slower read rates than bar code systems and are priced about the same. OCR systems are attractive when both human- and machine-readable capabilities are required.

Until recently, the commercial applications of optical character recognition have been confined to document reading and limited use for merchandise tag reading at the retail point of sale. Without tight control of character printing and the reading environment, OCR's **performance** has not met the criteria established by other automatic identification techniques. A single printing anomaly, such as an ink spot or void can easily obscure or transpose an OCR character - rendering the label unreadable or liable to misreading. Where encoding space is at a premium and the environment is relatively contaminant-free, OCR may be a viable alternative.

In Japanese book stores a small ticket with optical characters identifying the title, author, publisher, price, and SKU is placed inside each book. Upon purchase at a retail outlet, the ticket is removed and mailed back to the book distributor. The tickets are accumulated on a daily basis and fed through a high-speed OCR reader to create picking waves that are released to the warehouse floor.

Radio Frequency Tags

Radio frequency (RF) tags encode data on a chip that is encased in a tag. When a tag is within range of a special antenna, the chip is decoded by a tag reader. RF tags can be programmable or permanently coded and can be read from up to 30 feet away. Surface acoustical wave (SAW) tags are permanently coded and can be read only within a 6-foot range.

RF tags are typically used for permanent identification of a container, where advantage can be taken of the tag's durability. RF tags are also attractive in harsh environments where printed codes may deteriorate and become illegible. A tag reader costs around $10,000. Non-programmable tags range in price from $8 to $50; programmable tags, from $50 to $150.

At a large textiles manufacturer, the contents of a truckload are encoded into a RF tag located in the windshield of the truck. The tag can be read by antennae placed at 10 mile increments along the highway to allow a customer to watch the progress of its load and to prelocate the contents of the truckload. This technology facilitates cross-docking and direct (no-staging) putaway of truckload contents to primary and reserve picking locations.

Magnetic Stripes

Magnetic stripes commonly appear on the back of credit or bank cards. They are used to store a large quantity of information in a small space. The magnetic stripe is readable through dirt or grease, and the data contained in the stripe can be changed. The stripe must be read by contact, thus eliminating high-speed sortation applications. Magnetic stripe systems are generally more expensive than bar code systems. In warehousing, magnetic stripes are used on smart cards in a variety of paperless applications. Smart cards are now used in warehousing to capture information ranging from employee identification, to the contents of a trailer load of material, to the composition of an order picking tour. For example, at a large cosmetics distribution center order picking tours are downloaded onto smart cards. The smart cards are in turn inserted into a smart card reader built into each order picking cart. In so doing, the picking tour is illuminated on an electronic map of the warehouse appearing on the front of the cart.

Automatic, Paperless Communication Systems

Automatic identification media by itself does not yield paperless warehousing. We also need paperless communication systems to communicate what has been automatically identified.

The variety of paperless communication systems in warehousing is proliferating and now includes radio frequency data communication, light directed transactions, smart cards, voice input/output, and vision systems.

Radio Frequency Data Communication

Handheld, lift-truck mounted, and hands-free radio data terminals (RDTs) (Figure 5.5) are rapidly emerging as reliable tools for both inventory and vehicle/driver management. RDTs incorporate a multi-character display, full keyboard and special function keys. They communicate and receive messages on a prescribed frequency via strategically located antennae and a host computer interface unit. Beyond the basic thrust toward tighter control of inventory, improved resource utilization is most often cited in justification of these devices. Further, the increasing availability of software packages that permit RDT linkage to existing plant or warehouse control systems greatly simplify their implementation. The majority of RDTs installed in plants and warehouses use handheld wands or scanners for data entry, product identification, and location verification. This marriage of technologies provides higher levels of speed, accuracy, and productivity than could be achieved by either technology alone.

Figure 5.5a Vehicle-Mounted Radio Frequency Terminal [Telxon].

Figure 5.5b Handheld Radio Frequency Terminal with
Integrated Scanner .

Figure 5.5c Handsfree Radio Frequency Terminal and Scanner [LXE].

Light-Directed Transactions

Light-directed operations (Figure 5.6) use indicator lights and lighted alphanumeric displays to direct warehouse operators in order picking, putaway, and/or sortation. The most popular use is in broken case picking from flow racks, shelving, and/or carousels. In the case of flow rack or bin shelving, a light display is placed at the front of each pick location (in the place of a location label). The light is illuminated if a pick is required from that location. The number of units to pick appears on the same display or on a display at the top of the flow rack or shelving bay. A typical light display system costs in the range of $100 to $200 per SKU position. Typical picking rates are in the range of 300 to 600 lines per person-hour and accuracy is in the range of 99.97%. In incremental justification, these rates and accuracies must pay for the incremental computer hardware and software costs.

Figure 5.6 Light-Directed Picking System [Kingston-Warren].

In carousels, a light tree is placed in front of each carousel. A light display appears on the tree to correspond to every picking level on the carousel. As a carrier is positioned in front of the order picker, the light display corresponding to the level to be picked from is illuminated. A typical light tree for carousel picking costs in the range of $100,000. However, if we normalize the cost by the number of items on a typical carousel, say 5,000, then the cost per SKU position is only $20.

Lights can also be used to direct case picking and pallet storage and retrieval operations.

Voice Input/Output

The use of synthesized voice (Figure 5.7) is increasingly popular in warehouse operations. In stationary systems, a synthesized voice is used to direct a stationary warehouse operator. For example, at a wholesale grocery distribution center, carousel operators are directed by lights and a broadcast synthesized voice speaks the correct picking location and quantity.

In mobile voice-based systems warehouse operators wear a headset with an attached microphone. Via synthesized voice, the WMS talks the operator through a series of transactions. For example, for a pallet putaway, the lift truck operator hears a command to putaway a particular pallet into a particular warehouse location. When the transaction is complete, the operator speaks, "putaway complete" into the microphone. Then the system speaks the

Figure 5.7 Voice Headset System [Vocollect].

next transaction to the operator. If the operator forgets the transaction, he simply speaks, "repeat transaction" and the system repeats the instruction.

The advantages of voice-based systems include hands and eyes-free operations, the operator's eyes are free from terminals or displays, and the system functions whether or not the operator is literate. Another advantage is the ease with which the system is programmed. A simple *Windows*-based software package is used to construct all necessary transaction conversations. To operate every area of the warehouse with a voice-based system would require conversations for receiving, putaway, restocking, order picking, and shipping. Once those conversations have been developed, the system is a WMS unto itself. This approach can be an inexpensive way to achieve a majority of the functionality of a typical WMS. A typical mobile, voice-based system costs approximately the same as a RDT-based system, in the range of $3,000 to $5,000 per terminal.

Vision Systems

Vision system cameras take pictures of objects and codes and send the pictures to a computer for interpretation. Vision systems "read" at moderate speeds, with excellent accuracy at least for limited environments. Obviously, these systems do not require contact with the object or code. However, the accuracy of a read is highly dependent on the quality of light. Vision systems are becoming less costly but are still relatively expensive.

A large mail order operator recently installed a vision system at receiving. The system is located above a telescoping conveyor used to convey inbound cartons from a trailer into the warehouse. The system recognizes those inbound cartons that do not have bar codes, reads the product and vendor number on the carton, and directs a bar code printer to print and apply the appropriate bar code label.

Selecting and Justifying Paperless Warehousing Systems

An incremental justification approach should be used in selecting and justifying paperless warehousing systems. A critical distinction is the difference between real-time and paperless. There are paperless systems that are not real-time. For example, there are batch-oriented bar code scanning systems and batch-oriented mobile voice-based systems. Consequently, the benefits of paperless and real-time communications must be documented separately, otherwise the justification will be flawed.

Selecting, Justifying, and Implementing Warehouse Management Systems

The process of selecting, justifying, and implementing a warehouse management system (WMS) can raise a warehouse to world-class status or set the operation back ten years. Rarely is there anything in the middle. It is risky for the business and for your career as well. Here's a little advice for your trip down this rocky road.

WMS Selection

The WMS selection process begins with the decision to build or buy the system. The pros and cons of building and buying warehouse management systems are summarized in Table 5.1 below.

If you decide to buy a system, remember that there are over 400 suppliers of WMS applications. Even the largest of these suppliers does less than $25 million per year in sales. Hence, all WMS vendors are by definition small companies. Selecting a supplier is treacherous business. This point registered with me loud and clear during a marketability assessment of a large supplier's WMS. The functional evaluation is illustrated in Figure 5.8. The technical evaluation is illustrated in Figure 5.9.

Issue	Buy	Build	It Depends
Initial Expense	Initial WMS expense is lower through large package suppliers since their development expense is leveraged against many clients.		
Maintenance Expense			If the in-house staff is highly competent in WMS, then the in-house maintenance may be more timely and less expensive. Otherwise, a package supplier will be less expensive and perhaps the only feasible alternative.
Customization		The world's best warehouse management systems were all built in-house. Customization of world-class operating principles to unique industry settings is the key. If warehousing is a key to your competitiveness, customization is critical.	
Responses to Changes			If the in-house staff is highly competent in WMS, then the in-house changes will be more timely and less expensive. Otherwise, a package supplier will be less expensive and perhaps the only feasible alternative.

Table 5.1 WMS Buy vs. Build Decision Issues.

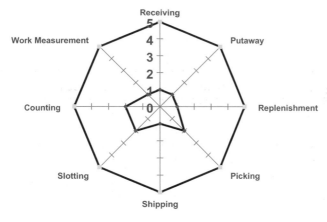

Figure 5.8 WMS Functional Evaluation.

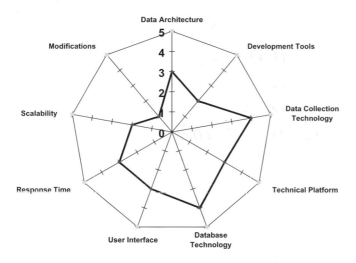

Figure 5.9 WMS Technical Evaluation.

In this case the functionality of the system is poor, yet the technical capability of the system is above average. Would you choose this system to support your pursuit of world-class warehousing? I hope not! If the system will only support stage 1, no-class processes, you can expect similar processes and performance in your warehouse - no matter how great the technology is!

Just like you can't judge a book by its cover; you can't judge software by its interface (or marketing literature). Nearly every WMS vendor offers GUI interfaces, object-oriented designs, full-featured functionality, a grade-A client listing, etc. To choose the right system and supplier you must "get under the hood to inspect the engine." You must meet the system designers. You must talk with the dissatisfied as well as the satisfied clients. You must learn about the origin of the system. (Many warehousing systems evolved from applications very far removed from warehousing including accounting, customer service, general ledger, inventory management, and/or manufacturing.) You must meet with the engineers and analysts who will be assigned to your project. (For most WMS vendors, there are few highly qualified engineers and analysts. Those few are typically assigned to the largest and most prestigious accounts. If you are not included in that list, you may not be satisfied with the capabilities of the engineers and analysts assigned to your project.)

Another key decision in selecting a WMS vendor is whether or not to work with a provider of integrated solutions. Those providers typically provide a full suite of business applications including customer service, purchasing, inventory management, general ledger, accounting, manufacturing management, and warehousing. Unfortunately, warehousing is typically an afterthought application for these providers and the full-suite providers typically have very little expertise in warehousing. Instead, I strongly recommend an approach that incorporates world-class warehouse management functionality. If you are serious about achieving world-class warehousing, there is no other option. As an alternative to the integrated solution approach, I typically recom-

Just like you can't judge a book by its cover; you can't judge software by its interface (or marketing literature).

Many warehousing systems evolved from applications very far removed from warehousing including accounting, customer service, general ledger, inventory management, and/or manufacturing.

mend the best-of-breed solution approach illustrated in Figure 5.10. This client-server logistics solution was developed for a large textiles company. The centerpiece is a relational and object-oriented logistics database. The database is designed around logistics objects and is continuously updated in real-time. Information on customers, items, orders, carriers, shipments, and manufacturing schedules is included in the database. Attached to the database are best-of-breed systems for customer response, manufacturing, warehousing, and transportation. It is impossible to achieve world-class logistics without world-class logistics systems!

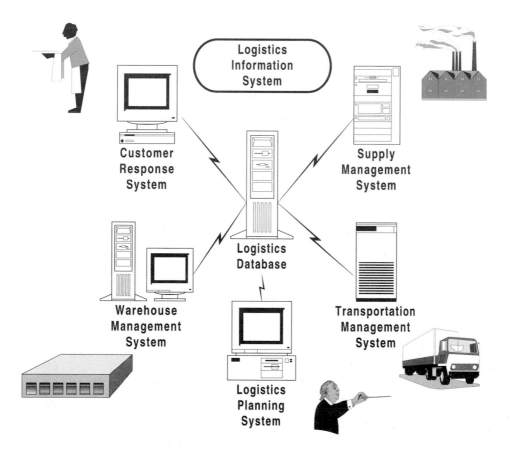

Figure 5.10 Logistics Information System Architecture.

WMS JUSTIFICATION

I was recently invited by a large heavy machinery company to conduct a seminar on bar coding. Unfortunately, I know very little about bar coding. I explained that to the client and asked curiously if the real topic was bar coding or the benefits of bar coding. Immediately the client explained that they wanted to learn about the benefits of bar coding including improved productivity, shipping and inventory accuracy, response time, and storage density. I was then able to explain that I knew a lot about how to make those improvements and that bar coding might or might not be on the road to those improvements.

We recently designed a WMS impact analysis for a client to help them focus on the fundamental benefits of computerizing warehouse operations. The WMS impact analysis chart (Table 5.2) has a column for each WKPI and a row for each feature that could not be achieved without the new system. If the feature could be achieved with alternative means, it can not be included on the chart. The impact, (positive or negative), in words, numbers, and direction of each new system feature is recorded in the cells of the matrix. The quantified, summarized, and annualized benefits of the new system are recorded in the last row of the chart. From the estimated annual benefits and the corporate payback period requirement, the justifiable system investment is derived. From that point on the project must be managed to that budget.

Activity	Current Practice	New practice	Productivity Impact	Storage Density Impact	Accuracy Impact	Response Time Impact
INBOUND						
1. Unload & Stage	Manual paperbased, CBLT with lift truck push-pull attachment. Place unirt loads on pallets for putaway.	Major change is license plate scanning. Lot mixing on a storage pallet Should not be permitted today.	Elimination of paperwork should offset additional scanning. Additional sorting of mixed SKU/ code date pallets is good discipline and should be done today.	No more mixed SKUs on a pallet. Need 1/4 and 1/2 pallet opening to minimize the impact. Need additional area for pallet decomposition.		
2. Check, Match, Tag	Manual, paperbased. Paperwork prepared and receipts prelocated.	Real-time paperless. Eliminates marual checking, matching, and tagging. All key entry eliminated.	1+office worker per DC. Won't send putaway operator to ooccupied location.		All key entry eliminated.	Takes 20 to 30 minutes out of the process per trailer.
3. Putaway	NAV transport to drop location and/or putaway. Paper-directed	RF-directed. Extra scanning.	Less likely to send cperators to occupied locations. Eliminattion of paper should offset additional scanning.		Location verification required.	
4. Interleaving	Not permitted	Permitted via real-time communication and real-time redirection of operators.	Empty travel time is significantly reduced.			Empty travel time is significantly reduced.
5. Cross-docking	Not permitted	Permitted via real-time directions to stage at shipping docks.	Critical capability for backorders. FIFO requirements limit opportunities.			

Table 5.2 WMS Impact Analysis Chart.

Activity	Current Practice	New practice	Productivity Impact	Storage Density Impact	Accuracy Impact	Response Time Impact
OUTBOUND						
1. Pallet to Door Picking	Paper-directed NAV retrieval and drop. Checker verifies SKU, lot, quantity, and applies move tag. Transporter moves pallet to shipping dok.	**RF-directed NAV retrieval and transport to shipping dock or drop zone.**	Increased single handling. Checking step eliminated. Real-time operator redirection.	Pick location verification. Location is available as soon as location is emptied.	Pick location verification.	
2. Replenishment to Bulk Picking Line	Paper-directed NAV drops pallet. Day's pick quantity transferred to empty pallet. Remainder to home location. Checker verifies SKU, lot, quantity, and applies move label.	RF-directed retrieval and move to dedicated position on case picking line.	Eliminates case picking to partial pallet. Eliminates putaway for remainder pallet. Eliminates bringing empty pallet to drop location.	Elimination of remainder pallet that previously occupied full storage location.	Pick confirmation.	
3. Partial Pallet Picking	Paper-directed, pick-to-pallet jack. No Pallet build sequencing.	RF-directed. Transactions sequenced heavy to light to coincide with pick line layout.	Sequenced transactions should increase productivity. Key will be to maintain handsfree picking.		Improved via location confirmation.	
4. Checking	Manual check of outbound loads for load sequence and pick quality.	Pick quantity verified at picking. Load sequenced verified on move.	Manual checking function virtually eliminated.			Manual checking function virtually eliminated.
5. Loading	Manual loading via CBLT.	Manual loading via CBLT.				
Work Measurement	Standards on 60+ transactions.	Time & date stamping for all transactions facilitates performance measurement.				

Table 5.2 WMS Impact Analysis Chart.

Activity	Current Practice	New practice	Productivity Impact	Storage Density Impact	Accuracy Impact	Response Time Impact
OVERALL			- Should permit a 10% to 20% productivity improvement per RDC. - If the planned training program is properly implemented, the learning curve should be no more than 3 months.	- Single SKU/code date per LP should increase space requirements. However, this practice should be followed today. 1/4 and 1/2 pallet openings should minimize the impact. - Shallow racking for returns storage should improve density. - Real-time, directed putaway will improve effective location utilization.	- Putaway and pick location verification will improve picking and inventory accuracy.	- Elimination of manual inbound checking, matching, and tagging.

Table 5.2 WMS Impact Analysis Chart.

WMS Implementation

Less than half of all warehouse management systems yield the performance and practice improvements promised during the justification phase. A major reason is that in many cases the implementation process is flawed. One flawed approach is the big bang approach in which an operation tries to leap in one-step from a highly manual operation to a fully automated and integrated solution. There are several major problems with this approach. First, it takes so long that many of the problems the system was originally designed to address have disappeared when it is time to implement. Second, many of the people involved in the selection and justification process will not be around to be involved in the implementation. Third, many of the benefits required to pay for the system occur after most of the investment has been made. Also, many of the benefits used to justify the system might be available for a much lower investment and in much less time than the big bang approach.

One flawed approach is the big bang approach in which an operation tries to leap in one-step from a highly manual operation to a fully automated and integrated solution.

In a recent project (Figure 5.11) we incrementally justified and implemented a full logistics information system. We began with the design of an object-oriented, relational logistics database and a definition of the ideal, fully integrated logistics information system. Once the database was populated, we attached PC-based profiling and decision support systems for warehousing (voice headset system), customer response, forecasting, inventory planning, and manufacturing. Based on the logistics gap analysis performed to justify the project, 50% of the projected benefits accrued from the first phase of the project. The first phase required only 10% of the projected investment requirements. In the second phase, the next logical system integration steps were taken as the PC-based warehousing and customer response systems were integrated into one client-server application and the forecasting, inventory planning, and manufacturing applications were integrated into another client-server application. These two applications were linked through real time updates to/from an object-relational logistics database. This phase brought another 30% of the projected benefits for another 30% of the anticipated investment. As a result, less than 1 year into the project, 80% of the projected benefits had been realized for less than 40% of the anticipated investment. No further integration was justifiable on an incremental basis.

Another flaw in the big-bang approach is that the associated re-engineering is typically done in series. Processes are redesigned, supporting systems are designed and implemented, and people are trained. Unfortunately it is not until people begin to implement the new processes that the project benefits are realized. Instead, the processes should be redesigned, the supporting systems designed and implemented, and the people trained in parallel. I recently developed a re-engineering process called *ConsulCation* to train the members of a cross-functional team as they work to redesign their warehousing and logistics processes. Simultaneously, the LIS infrastructure and PC-based profiling and decision support tools are being developed. This infrastructure and the PC-based tools serve as the springboard for more robust and integrated systems.

Unfortunately it is not until people begin to implement the new processes that the project benefits are realized.

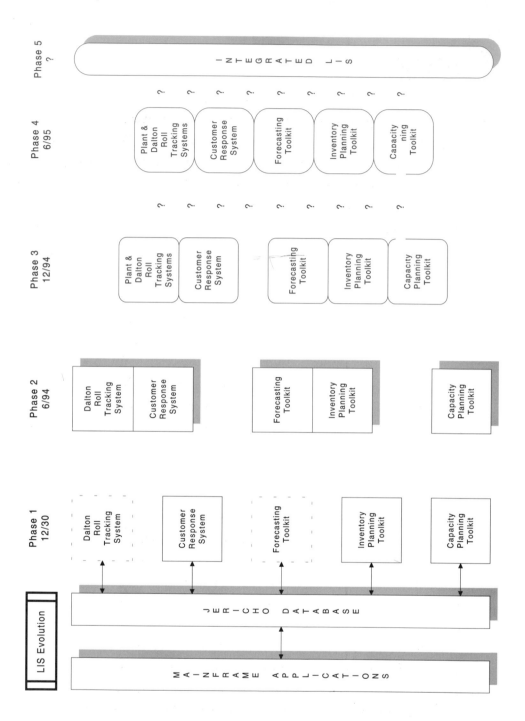

Figure 5.11 Logistics Information Systems Evolution Plan [The Progress Group].

5.3
SUMMARY

A warehouse management system permiting paperless ware-housing transactions is one of the necessary (but not suffi-cient) enablers for world-class warehousing. To try to achieve world-class warehousing without a world-class WMS is like trying to win the Indianapolis 500 on a bicycle. Many of the world-class warehousing practices described here cannot be achieved without the support of highly functional and flexible warehouse management systems.

To try to achieve world-class warehousing without a world-class WMS is like trying to win the Indianapolis 500 on a bicycle.

In this chapter we reviewed the technologies of paperless warehousing including automatic identication media and automatic, paperless communication systems. The world-class warehouse will have a variety of these technologies connected to a warehouse information highway. Paperless warehousing is rapidly becoming the rule as opposed to the exception.

We concluded this chapter with tips and techniques for selecting, implementing and justifying warehouse manage-ment systems. The key decision and design principles are *incremental justification* and *incremental implementation*. Incre-mental justification forces a systematic, and objective finan-cial justification of a warehouse management system. The principle was illustrated in the WMS impact analysis which assesses the contribution of each WMS feature to improve-ments in the warehouse key performance indicators. Incre-mental implementation is used to yield cost savings in the early, middle, and late stages of a WMS project to allow a project to pay for itself during each project phase.

MECHANIZING
WAREHOUSE OPERATIONS

After profiling the warehouse operations to identify root causes of operational problems and potential breakthrough process redesigns; benchmarking performance, practices, and infrastructure against world-class standards to set operational goals and to target justifiable investment; simplifying the operations by eliminating and streamlining as much material and information handling as possible; and computerizing the operations by leveraging computer hardware and software to automate information handling and to support profiling, benchmarking, and process simplification; we are ready to consider mechanizing the warehouse operations. Mechanization is considered late in the re-engineering game because mechanized systems are inherently complex, inflexible, and expensive. All of the warehouse re-engineering principles applied thus far have been aimed at simplifying the operations, making them more flexible, and minimizing fixed investments. However, after we have applied these principles, there is inevitably an important and justifiable role for mechanized systems in warehousing operations.

In some cases because of extreme throughput spikes, highly expensive land and/or labor, and/or severe shortages of land and/or labor, there is no other option than to utilize highly mechanized systems to achieve the mission of the warehouse.

In some cases because of extreme throughput spikes, highly expensive land and/or labor, and/or severe shortages of land and/or labor, there is no other option than to utilize highly mechanized systems to achieve the mission of the warehouse. In those cases and under more typical design scenarios, success with mechanization is a function of awareness of the full range of mechanization options and application of reliable selection and justification methods. That is the objective of this chapter, to introduce you to the full range of mechanization options for storing and retrieving pallets, cases, and loose items and to describe the pros, cons, costs, and appropriate application of each system.

This is not meant to be a full treatment of the material handling system alternatives for warehouse operations. Please consult [16, 17, 18, 19, 20] for a full treatment of those options. Instead, this chapter is organized along the lines of the principle handling units in warehousing - pallets, cases, and loose items (see Figure 6.1). A description of each material handling method for each handling unit is provided. In addition, a summary comparison and selection table is provided at the end of each section to help you in the selection and justification process.

200

The chapter begins with pallet storage and retrieval systems since their size often dictates the configuration of the rest of the operation. From there we will follow the decomposition of a typical unit load of storage. In every section we will begin with the least expensive, least complex system and build to the most expensive, most sophisticated alternative. The alternatives are presented in this order to reinforce the incremental justification principle - there must be enough incremental benefits stemming from a more expensive and sophisticated alternative to pay for the incremental costs and complexities.

There must be enough incremental benefits stemming from a more expensive and sophisticated alternative to pay for the incremental costs and complexities.

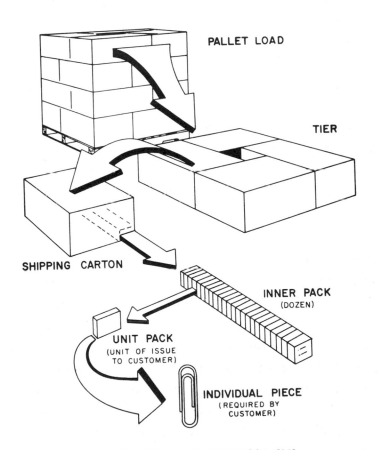

Figure 6.1 Unit Load Decomposition [25].

PALLET STORAGE AND RETRIEVAL SYSTEMS

This description of pallet storage and retrieval systems is organized under sub-headings with the same names - pallet storage systems and pallet retrieval systems. Though the decisions are interdependent, the storage system selection is driven primarily by the concern for improved storage density and is dictated by the on-hand inventory and turnover of the items in pallet storage. The retrieval system selection is driven primarily by the concern for high handling productivity and tradeoffs in required capital investment.

PALLET STORAGE SYSTEMS

The most popular pallet storage systems are:
- block stacking,
- stacking frames,
- single-deep selective pallet rack,
- double-deep rack,
- drive-in rack,
- drive-thru rack,
- pallet flow rack, and
- push-back rack.

Each alternative - its pros, cons, and related costs - is described below.

WORLD-CLASS WAREHOUSING © EDWARD H. FRAZELLE PH.D.

Block Stacking

Block stacking (Figure 6.2) refers to unit loads stacked on top of each other and stored on the floor in storage lanes (blocks) 2 to 10 loads deep. Depending on the weight and stability of the loads, the stacks may range from 2 loads high to a height determined by acceptable safe limits, load stackability, vehicle lift height capacity, the crushability of the loads, and/or the building clear height. Loads in a block should be retrieved under a LIFO (last-in-first-out) discipline. Hence, if highly sensitive (more strict than lot or code date) FIFO requirements are in place, block stacking is not a feasible storage method. Block stacking is particularly effective when there are multiple pallets per SKU (stock keeping unit) and when inventory is turned in large increments i.e. several loads of the same SKU are received or withdrawn at one time.

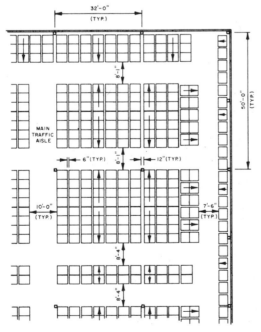

Figure 6.2 Block Stacking Layout [25].

As loads are removed from a storage lane, a space-loss phenomenon referred to as *honeycombing* (Figure 6.3) occurs with block stacking. Since only one SKU can be effectively stored in a lane, empty pallet spaces are created which cannot be utilized effectively until an entire lane is emptied. Therefore, in order to maintain high utilization of the available storage positions, the lane depth (number of loads stored from the aisle) must be carefully determined. (The slotting module in the *Warehouse Toolbox* makes these computations based on formulas provided in [21].) Because no racking is required, the investment in a block stacking system is low. Block stacking is easy to implement, and it allows near-infinite flexibility for floorspace configuration.

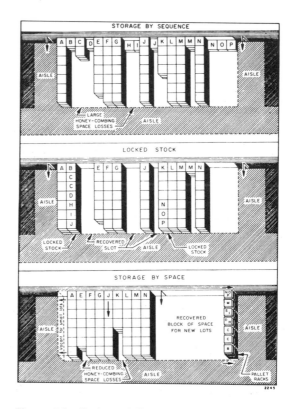

Figure 6.3a Horizontal Honeycombing Losses [25].

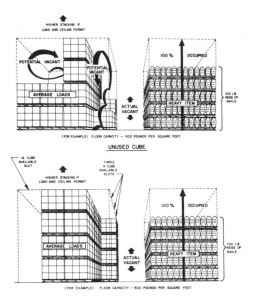

Figure 6.3b Vertical Honeycombing Losses [25].

Pallet Stacking Frames

Pallet stacking frames (Figure 6.4) are either frames attached to standard wooden pallets or self-contained steel units made up of decks and posts. Stacking frames are portable and enable the user to stack material several loads high. When not in use, the frames can be disassembled and stored in a minimum amount of space.

Stacking frames are commonly used when loads are not stackable and when other racking alternatives are not justifiable. Also, since stacking frames can be leased, they are popular when there is a short-term spike in inventory and the frames are needed to increase storage density in what is normally open floorspace.

A single stacking frame costs between $100 and $300. All of the storage density losses due to honeycombing described earlier for block stacking also apply to stacking frames.

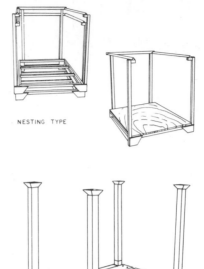

NESTING TYPE

Figure 6.4 Pallet Stacking Frame.

Single-Deep Pallet Rack

Single-deep pallet racking (Figure 6.5) is a simple construction of metal uprights and cross-members providing immediate (pick-face) access to each load stored (i.e. no honeycombing). Unlike block stacking, when a pallet space is created by the removal of a load, a pallet opening is immediately available. Also, since racking is supporting every load, the stacking height is not limited by the stackability and/or crushability of the loads, and multiple SKUs can be stacked in the same vertical column (bay) of storage space.

Figure 6.5 Single-Deep Pallet Rack [25].

Loads do not need to be stackable and may be of varying heights and widths. In instances where the load depth is highly variable, it may be necessary to provide load supports or decking.

A typical single-deep rack position costs between $40 and $50. The major advantage is full accessibility to all unit loads. The major disadvantage is the amount of space devoted to aisles - typically 50% to 60% of the available floor space. As a result, in cases where there are three or more pallets on-hand of an SKU, a storage method that houses at least two pallets in a facing is preferrable.

The major advantage is full accessibility to all unit loads. The major disadvantage is the amount of space devoted to aisles - typically 50% to 60% of the available floor space.

Selective pallet rack might be considered as the "benchmark" storage mode, against which other systems may be compared for advantages and disadvantages. Most storage systems benefit from the use of at least some selective pallet rack for SKUs whose storage requirement is less than three to five pallet loads.

Double-Deep Pallet Rack

Double-deep pallet racks (Figure 6.6) are merely selective racks that are two pallet positions deep. The advantage of two-deep rack facings (perpendicular to the aisle) is that fewer aisles are needed. In most cases a 50% aisle space savings is achieved versus single-deep selective rack. However, we cannot assume that a 50% *true* space savings will be achieved since we can only anticipate a 70% to 75% utilization of the available openings (due to honeycombing). (80% to 85% utilization is common for single deep racking.)

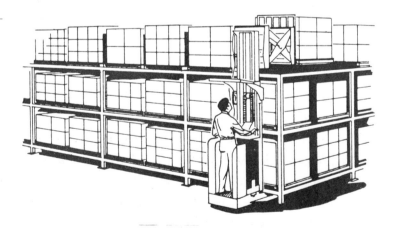

Figure 6.6 Double-Deep Pallet Rack.

Double deep racks are typically used when the storage requirement for an SKU is five pallets or greater and when product is received and picked frequently in multiples of two pallets. (Assigning SKUs with only a single pallet on-hand to double-deep racking is nonsensical since one of the two positions in a facing is automatically wasted.) Since pallets are stored two deep, a double reach fork lift is required for storage/retrieval.

Double deep racks are typically used when the storage requirement for an SKU is five pallets or greater and when product is received and picked frequently in multiples of two pallets.

Drive-In Rack

Drive-in racks (Figure 6.7) extend the reduction of aisle space begun with double-deep pallet rack by providing storage lanes from 5 to 10 loads deep and 3 to 5 loads high. Drive-in racks allow a lift truck to drive in to the rack several pallet positions and store or retrieve a pallet. This is possible because the rack consists of upright columns that have horizontal rails to support pallets at a height above that of the lift truck. This construction permits multiple levels of pallet storage, each level being supported independently of the others.

One drawback of drive-in rack is the reduction of lift truck travel speed needed for safe navigation within the confines of the rack construction. Another drawback is the honeycombing losses since no more than one SKU can be housed in a lane. As a result drive-in rack is best used for slow-to medium-velocity SKU's with 12 or more pallets on-hand. As was the case with block stacking, loads should be retrieved with a LIFO discipline and with a retrieval discipline to free up each lane as quickly as possible.

As a result drive-in rack is best used for slow to medium velocity SKUs with 12 or more pallets on-hand.

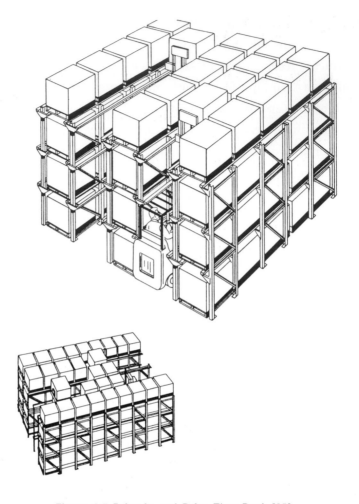

Figure 6.7 Drive-In and Drive-Thru Rack [25].

Drive-Thru Rack

Drive-thru rack is merely drive-in rack that is accessible from both sides of the rack. It is for staging loads in a flow-thru fashion were a pallet is loaded at one end and retrieved at the other end. The same considerations for drive-in rack apply to drive-thru rack.

Pallet Flow Rack

Functionally, pallet flow rack (Figure 6.8) is used like drive-thru rack. However, loads are conveyed (FIFO) on skate wheel conveyor, roller conveyor, or rails from one end of a storage lane to the other. As a load is removed from the front of a storage lane the next load advances to the pick face. The main purpose of pallet flow rack is to provide high throughput pallet storage and retrieval and good space utilization. Hence, it is used for those items with high pallet inventory turnover and with eight or more pallets on-hand. The major disadvantage of pallet flow rack is the expense; $200 to $300 per storage position.

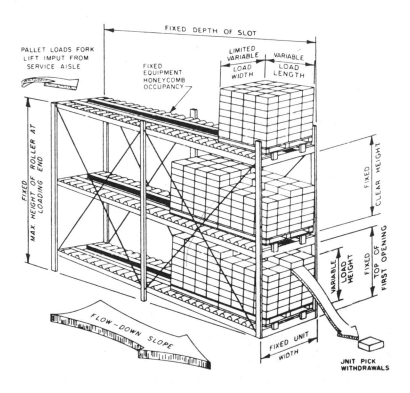

Figure 6.8 Pallet Flow Rack.

Push-Back Rack

Push-back rack (Figure 6.9) provides last-in-first-out, deep-lane (two to five pallets deep) storage using a rail-guided carrier for each pallet load. As a load is placed into storage, its weight and the force of the putaway vehicle pushes the other loads in the lane back into the lane to create room for the additional load. As a load is removed from the front of a storage lane, the weight of the remaining load automatically advances remaining loads to the rack face. Hence, every SKU has a load that is immediately accessible. In addition, since all of the putaway and retrieval takes place at the rack face, there is no need for special lift truck attachments as was the case with double-deep rack. An advantage over drive-in rack is that there is no need to drive into the rack and there is no vertical honeycombing. Push-back rack is appropriate for medium to fast-moving SKUs with three to ten pallets on-hand. The cost of typical push-back rack is in the range of $150 per pallet position.

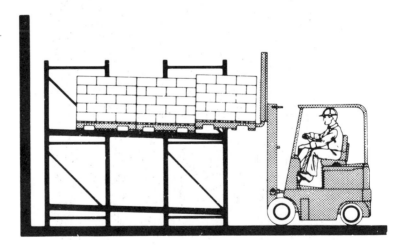

Figure 6.9 Push-Back Rack.

WORLD-CLASS WAREHOUSING © EDWARD H. FRAZELLE PH.D.

Mobile Pallet Rack

Mobile pallet racks (Figure 6.10) are essentially single-deep pallet racks on wheels or tracks permitting an entire row of racks to move away from adjacent rack rows. The underlying principal is that aisles are only justified when they are being used; the rest of the time they are occupying valuable space. Access to a particular storage row is achieved by moving (mechanically or manually) the adjacent row and creating an aisle in front of the desired row. As a result, less than 10% of the floorspace is devoted to aisles, and storage density is the highest of any of the pallet storage alternatives. Unfortunately, the pallet storage retrieval productivty is the lowest of any of the alternatives we have considered. Hence, mobile racks are justifiable when space is scarce and expensive, and for slow-moving SKUs with one to three pallets on-hand. The cost of typical mobile rack is in the range of $250 per pallet position.

Figure 6.10 Mobile Pallet Rack [White].

Pallet Storage Systems Selection

The key to selecting the appropriate pallet storage system configuration is to assign each SKU to a pallet storage system whose storage and productivity characteristics match the activity and inventory profile of the SKU. The table and figure below are designed to assist you in this matching process. Table 6.1 below is a summary of the key features of each pallet storage system including cost, storage density, load accessibility, throughput capacity, inventory and location control, FIFO maintenance, load size variability, and ease of installation. The letters A, B, C, D, and F correspond to the evaluations of excellent, above average, average, below average, and poor.

Figure 6.11 below illustrates an example pallet storage mode analysis. The example is taken from a particular case and cannot be generalized since the preference regions vary widely as a function of the cost and availability of labor and space. The analysis indicates the most economically appropriate assignment of popularity-inventory families to pallet storage modes.

PALLET RETRIEVAL SYSTEMS

The most popular pallet retrieval and putaway systems are:
- walkie stackers,
- counterbalance lift trucks,
- straddle trucks,
- straddle reach trucks,

Criteria	Floor Storage	Stacking Frame	Single-Deep	Double-Deep	Drive-In Rack	Drive-Thru	Flow Rack	Push-Back	Mobile Rack	Cantilever
Cost per Position	n/a	$50	$40	$50	$65	$65	$200	$150	$250	
Potential Storage Density	A	B	D	C	B	B	B	B	A	B
Load Access	F	F	A	C	B	B	B	A	F	A
Throughput Capacity	B	D	B	C	C	C	A	C	F	C
Inventory & Location Control	F	F	A	C	D	D	C	C	D	B
FIFO Maintenance	F	F	A	C	D	D	A	C	C	A
Ability to House Variable Load Sizes	A	D	C	C	D	D	F	C	C	B
Ease of Installation	A	A	C	C	C	C	F	C	F	B

Table 6.1 Pallet Storage Mode Selection and Evaluation Criteria.

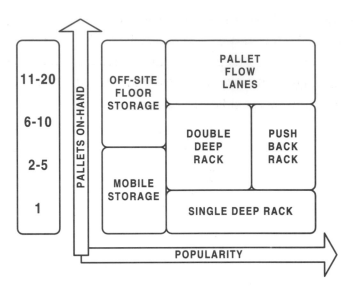

Figure 6.11 Example Pallet Storage Mode Economic Analysis
[Warehouse Toolbox].

·   sideloader trucks,
·   turret trucks,
·   hybrid trucks, and
·   automated storage and retrieval machines.

The applications, pros, cons, and related costs of each system are described below.

Walkie Stackers

A walkie stacker (Figure 6.12) allows a pallet to be lifted, stacked, and transported short distances. The operator steers from a walking position behind the vehicle. The walkie stacker may be appropriate in situations where there is low throughput, short travel distances, low vertical storage height, and a low cost solution is desired. A typical walkie stacker can stack loads a maximum of three loads high, costs in the range of $10,000, and can load/unload a truck and retrieve/putaway a pallet in the same move.

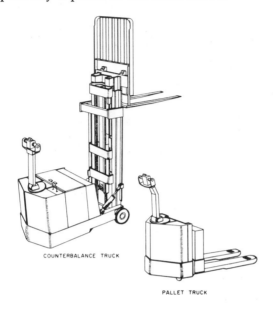

COUNTERBALANCE TRUCK

PALLET TRUCK

Figure 6.12 Walkie Stacker [25].

Counterbalanced Lift Trucks

As the name implies, counterbalance lift trucks (Figure 6.13) employ a counterbalance in the back of the truck to stabilize loads carried and lifted on a mast at the front of the truck. Counterbalance lift trucks may be gas or battery powered. Besides forks, other attachments may be used to lift unique load configurations on a vertical mast. The lift height limitation is generally around 25 feet. Counterbalance trucks are available with operating capacities up to 100,000 pounds and cost in the range of $30,000.

Figure 6.13 Sit-Down Counterbalance Lift Truck [25].

Counterbalance trucks also offer the flexibility to retrieve/putaway a pallet and load/unload a truck in the same move.

Since the operator rides (seated or standing in the case of stand-up counterbalance trucks) on the vehicle, counterbalance trucks can be used for longer moves than walkie stackers. Counterbalance trucks also offer the flexibility to retrieve/putaway a pallet and load/unload a truck in the same move. This flexibility, coupled with the vehicle's relatively low cost, make the counterbalance lift truck the benchmark for all other pallet retrieval vehicles.

The major drawback of the counterbalance lift truck is the wide turning radius required to turn the vehicle in an aisle. As a result, a 11' to 12' storage aisle width is typically required. This aisle width requirement is the justification focus of alternative vehicles. As we proceed through the remaining list, the vehicles will offer progressively narrower storage aisles (hence the reference to *narrow aisle vehicles*) and progressively higher reaching heights. At the same time, the vehicles become progressively more expensive and none offer the rack retrieval/putaway and truck load/unload flexibility that the counterbalance truck offers. Hence, the incremental space savings and cost must be sufficient to pay for the incremental vehicle cost and loss of handling flexibility.

Straddle Trucks

A straddle truck (Figure 6.14) provides load and vehicle stability by using outriggers to straddle the pallet load, instead of counterbalanced weight. As a result, the aisle width requirement is 8′ to 10′ as opposed to the 11′ to 12′ required by a counterbalance truck. To access loads in storage, the outriggers are driven into the rack allowing the mast to come flush with the pallet face. Hence, it is necessary to support the floor level load on rack beams. A typical straddle truck costs in the range of $35,000.

Figure 6.14 Straddle Truck [Crown].

Straddle Reach Trucks

Straddle reach trucks (Figure 6.15) were developed from conventional straddle trucks by shortening the outriggers on the straddle truck and providing a "reach" capability with a scissor reach mechanism. In so doing, the outriggers do not have to be driven under the floor level load to allow access to the storage positions. Hence, no rack beam is required at the floor level, conserving rack cost and vertical storage requirements.

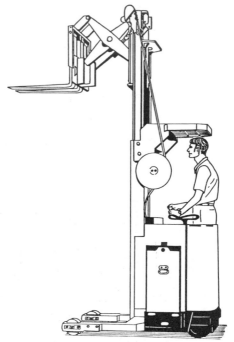

Figure 6.15 Straddle Reach Truck.

The major drawback of the sideloader truck is the need to enter the correct end of the aisle to access a particular location.

Two basic straddle reach truck designs are available: mast and fork reach trucks. The mast-reach design consists of a set of tracks along the outriggers that support the mast. The fork reach design consists of a pantograph or scissors mounted on the mast.

The double-deep reach truck, a variation of the fork reach design, allows the forks to be extended to a position that permits loads to be stored two deep. A typical straddle reach truck operates in a 8' to 10' aisle and costs in the range of $40,000.

Sideloading Trucks

Sideloading (or sideloader) trucks (Figure 6.16) load and unload from one side, thus eliminating the need to turn in the aisle to access storage positions. Hence, sideloading vehicles can operate in a 6' to 7' wide aisle.

There are two basic sideloader designs. Either the entire mast moves on a set of tracks transversely across the vehicle, or the forks project from a fixed mast on a pantograph.

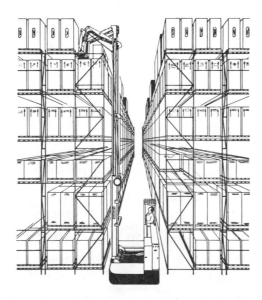

Figure 6.16   Sideloader Truck [25].

A variety of load types can be handled using a sideloader. The vehicle's configuration particularly lends itself to storing long loads in cantilever rack. Sideloaders can generally access loads up to 40 feet high and cost in the range of $75,000.

The major drawback of the sideloader truck is the need to enter the correct end of the aisle to access a particular location, thus adding to the time and complexity involved in truck routing. Turret trucks are designed to address this shortcoming while offering all of the other benefits of sideloader trucks.

Turret Trucks

Like sideloading trucks, turret trucks (Figure 6.17) (sometimes referred to as swingmasts or shuttle trucks) do not require the vehicle to make a turn within the aisle to store or retrieve a pallet. Instead, the load is lifted either by forks which swing on the mast, a mast which swings from the vehicle, or a shuttle fork mechanism.

Figure 6.17a Swing-Mast Turret Truck [25].

Figure 6.17b Swing-Fork Turret Truck [25].

Generally, these types of trucks provide access to load positions at heights up to 50 feet, and can operate in aisles 5 or 6 feet wide. Turret trucks generally have good maneuverability outside the aisle, and some of the designs with telescoping masts may be driven into a shipping trailer. The vehicle may be wire guided or the aisles may be rail guided, allowing for greater speed and safety in the aisle and reducing the chances of damage to the vehicle and/or rack. A typical turret truck costs in the range of $95,000.

Hybrid Storage/Retrieval Trucks

A hybrid S/R truck (Figure 6.18) is similar to a turret truck, except that the operator's cab is lifted with the load.

The hybrid truck evolved from the design of an automated storage and retrieval machine used in automated storage/retrieval systems (AS/RS). Unlike the AS/RS machine, a hybrid truck is not captive to an aisle, but may leave one aisle and enter another. Present models available are somewhat clumsy outside the aisle, but operate within the aisle at a high throughput rate.

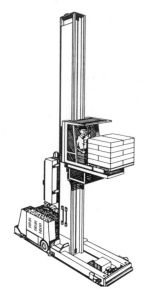

Figure 6.18 Hybrid Truck [25].

Hybrid trucks operate in aisle widths ranging from 5 to 7 feet, allow rack storage up to 60 feet high in a rack supported building, and may include an enclosed operator's cab which may be heated and/or air conditioned.

Sophisticated hybrid trucks are able to travel horizontally and vertically simultaneously to a load position. The lack of flexibility, the high capital commitment and high dimensional tolerance in the rack are the disadvantages of hybrid vehicles. The cost of a typical hybrid storage/retrieval truck is in the range of $125,000.

Automated Storage/Retrieval Systems

An automated storage/retrieval system (AS/RS) (Figure 6.19) for pallets is commonly referred to as a unit load AS/RS. It is defined by the AS/RS product section of the Material Handling Institute [22] as a storage system that uses fixed-path storage and retrieval (S/R) machines running on one or more rails between fixed arrays of storage racks.

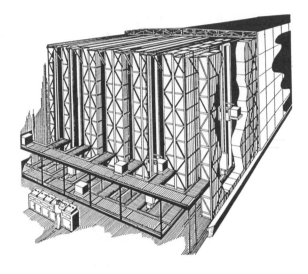

Figure 6.19 Automated Storage and Retrieval System [25].

A unit load AS/RS usually handles loads in excess of 1,000 pounds and is used for raw material, work-in-process, and finished goods. The number of systems installed in the United States is in the hundreds, and installations are commonplace in all major industries.

A typical AS/RS operation involves the S/R machine picking up a load at the front of the system, transporting the load to an empty location, depositing the load in the empty location, and returning empty to the input/output (I/O) point. Such an operation is called a single command (SC) operation. Single commands accomplish either a storage or a retrieval between successive visits to the I/O point. A more efficient operation is a dual command (DC) operation. A DC involves the S/R machine picking up a load at the I/O point, traveling loaded to an empty location (typically the closest empty location to the I/O point), depositing the load, traveling empty to the location of the desired retrieval, picking up the load, traveling loaded to the I/O point, and depositing the load. The key idea is that in a dual command, two operations, a storage and a retrieval, are accomplished between successive visits to the I/O point.

A unique feature of the S/R machine travel is that vertical and horizontal travel occur simultaneously. Consequently, the time to travel to any destination in the rack is the maximum of the horizontal and vertical travel times required to reach the destination from the origin. Horizontal travel speeds are on the order of 500 feet per minute; vertical, 120 feet per minute.

The typical unit load AS/RS in its most straightforward configuration includes unit loads stored one deep (i.e., single deep), in long narrow aisles, each of which contains a S/R machine. A single I/O point is located at the lowest level of storage and at one end of the system.

More often than not, one of the parameters defining the system is atypical. The possible variations include the depth of storage, the number of S/R machines assigned to an aisle, and the number and location of I/O points. These variations are described in more detail below.

When the variety of loads stored in the system is relatively low, throughput requirements are moderate to high, and the number of loads to be stored is high, it is often beneficial to store loads more than one deep in the rack. Alternative configurations include:

- Double deep storage with single-load width aisles. Loads of the same stock-keeping unit (SKU) are typically stored in the same location. A modified S/R machine is capable of reaching into the rack for the second load.

- Double deep storage with double-load-width aisles. The S/R machine carries two loads at a time and inserts them simultaneously into the double deep cubicle.

- Deep lane storage with single-load-width aisles. An S/R machine dedicated to putaway transactions stores material in storage lanes on either side of the aisle. A lane may hold up to 10 loads each. On the output side, a dedicated retrieval machine removes material from the storage lanes.

- Rack entry module (REM) systems in which a REM moves into the rack system and places/receives loads onto/from special rails in the rack.

Another variation of the typical configuration is the use of transfer cars to transport S/R machines between aisles. Transfer cars are used when the storage requirement is high relative to the throughput requirement. In such a case, the throughput requirement does not justify the purchase of an S/R machine for each aisle, yet the number of aisles of storage must be sufficient to accommodate the storage requirement.

A third system variation is the number and location of I/O points. Throughput requirements or facility design constraints may mandate multiple I/O points at locations other than the lower left hand corner of the rack. Multiple I/O points might be used to separate inbound and outbound loads and/or to provide additional throughput capacity. Alternative I/O locations include the type of the system at the end of the rack (some AS/RS are built underground) and the middle of the rack.

A typical AS/RS machine costs in the range of $300,000.

Pallet Retrieval Systems Selection

Table 6.2 below summarizes the key storage and handling features of each of the pallet retrieval system options. Table 6.2 and Table 6.1 should be used jointly to determine the appropriate pallet storage and retrieval systems configuration for a warehouse. The Warehouse Toolbox™ described earlier considers each item in each storage and retrieval system to recommend an optimal storage-retrieval system combination for each item.

	Counter-balance	Straddle	Straddle Reach	Sideloader	Turret	Hybrid	ASRS
Vehicle Cost	$30,000	$35,000	$40,000	$75,000	$95,000	$125,000	$200,000
Lift Height Capacity	22`	21`	30`	30`	40`	50`	75`
Aisle Width	10-12`	7-9`	6-8`	5-7`	5-7`	5`	4.5`
Weight Capacity	2-10k	2-6k	2-5k	2-10k	3-4k	2-4k	2-5k
Lift Speed	80 fpm	60 fpm	50 fpm	50 fpm	75 fpm	60 fpm	100 fpm
Travel Speed	550 fpm	470 fpm	490 fpm	440 fpm	490 fpm	490 fpm	500 fpm

Table 6.2 Pallet Retrieval Systems Comparison.

6.2
CASE PICKING SYSTEMS

The alternative case picking systems include pallet jack picking, order picker trucks, pick-to-conveyor, end-of-aisle AS/RS, layer picking, and automated dispensing. The pros, cons, applications, and related cost of each alternative are described below and are summarized in Table 6.3 which concludes the section.

PALLET JACK PICKING

A pallet jack (Figure 6.20) is a motorized vehicle equipped with forks to transport pallets at floor-level. The operator rides on the front of the vehicle with the pallet secured by the forks on the back of the vehicle. A double pallet jack can carry two pallets at a time. Pallet jacks are by far the most popular method for case picking, and are so common in the grocery industry that pallet jack picking is often referred to as the grocery picking method.

Figure 6.20 Double Pallet Jack [25].

The advantages of pallet jack picking are the low capital investment required, the simplicity of the concept, flexibility, and safety since all of the picking takes place at floor level. Typical pallet jack picking rates range between 150 and 250 cases per person-hour. The cost of a typical pallet jack is around $8,000.

ORDER PICKER TRUCKS

Order picker trucks (Figure 6.21), sometimes referred to as stock pickers or cherry pickers, allow the order picker to travel to pick locations well above floor level. Since vertical travel velocity is much slower than horizontal travel velocity, and since the operator must take special care in positioning the vehicle in front of the pick location, the productivity of case picking with an order picker truck is only in the range of 50 to 100 cases per person-hour. (The productivity can be enhanced by minimizing vertical travel through popularity-based storage and/or intelligent pick tour construction.) Hence, order picker trucks are usually used for picking slower moving items and where high density storage is required. A typical order picker truck costs approximately $30,000.

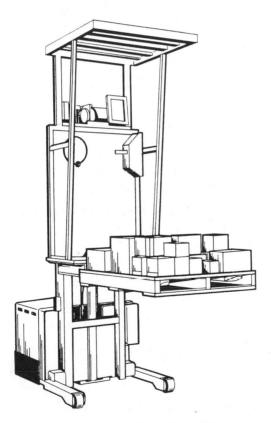

Figure 6.21 Order Picker Truck [25].

PICK-TO-CONVEYOR

In case pick-to-conveyor operations (Figure 6.22) a conveyor runs the length of the case picking line allowing the order picker to walk down the line removing cases from pallet storage locations and placing them on a takeaway belt or roller conveyor. Typically the operator applies a bar code label to each case as he removes it from its storage location. The bar code label is used for carton identification and downstream sortation of each case into its customer order.

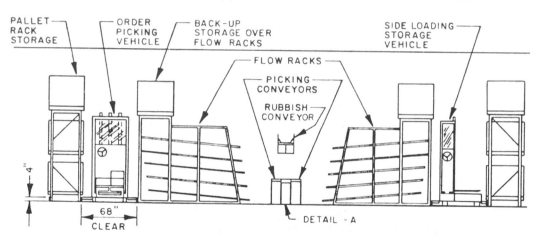

Figure 6.22 Case-Pick-to-Conveyor Operation.

The advantage of pick-to-conveyor operations (over pallet and order picker trucks) is a substantial increase in picking productivity, a result of pickers being confined to zones, less travel distance between picks, and the elimination of the order picker palletizing as they pick. The disadvantage is the need for a downstream sortation system. Hence, there must be enough incremental productivity increase (pick-to-conveyor vs. pallet jack picking) to pay for the additional mechanization required.

Tier (or Layer) Picking

Full tier or layer picking systems (Figure 6.23) are used to mechanically extract an entire layer of cases from a pallet. There are a variety of mechanical approaches for layer picking including (1) vacuum suction and conveyor singulation of the top layer, (2) four-sided clamping and conveyor singulation, and (3) layer stripping conveyors which literally lift up the front edge of the top layer and strip it away from the remaining layers. The advantage of layer picking over the other case picking methods is the total elimination of human handling of the cases and high case handling capacity. A typical layer picker can handle between 750 and 1000 cases per hour. The disadvantage is the high degree of mechanization and associated cost. As a result, layer pickers can typically only be justified when customers tend to order in high-volume, layer quantities and when the cost of labor is high.

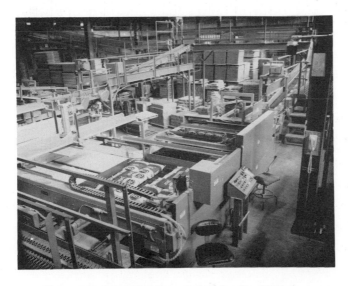

Figure 6.23 Automated De-palletizer for Tier Picking.

END-OF-AISLE AS/RS

Though rare, in some cases automated storage and retrieval systems (Figure 6.24) are used to automatically convey pallet quantities to a stationary operator. The operator transfers the required number of cases from the storage pallet to the order pallet. Both pallets can be positioned such that the top of the pallet is at or near waist level for ease of handling. The advantages include high storage density of the storage pallets, excellent ergonomics, and relatively high productivity since the operators are stationary. The disadvantages are the high degree of mechanization required and the associated capital investment and control complexities.

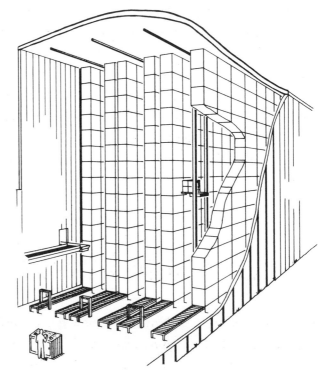

Figure 6.24 End-of-Aisle Automated Storage and Retrieval System.

AUTOMATED CASE DISPENSING

Automated case dispensing systems (Figure 6.25) can be used to fully automate the putaway and retrieval of individual cases. In some systems, the cases are housed in gravity flow racks. A shuttle table and a telescoping conveyor are attached to a vertical mast that travels on rails along the picking/putaway face. For putaway, a transport conveyor feeds individual cases to the telescoping conveyor. The cases travel up and along the telescoping conveyor to the putaway location. The shuttle table rides up the mast and horizontally with the mast to the putaway location. The telescoping conveyor feeds cases to the shuttle table which in turn inserts cases in a gravity flow rack lane. The picking process is the putaway process in reverse. The advantage of automated case dispensing is the complete elimination of human operators and the related labor and workman's compensation costs. The major drawback is the high maintenance requirements and the high initial investment. Each automated case dispensing mechanism costs approximately $500,000. An automated case dispensing mechanism can dispense approximately 500 cases per hour.

CASE PICKING SYSTEMS SELECTION

A formal economic case picking mode analysis should be conducted to identify the appropriate combination of case picking systems. This analysis should consider the activity and inventory profile of each item and the storage and

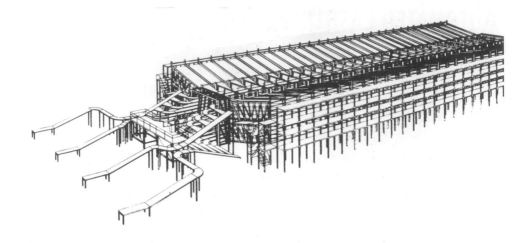

Figure 6.25 Automated Case Dispensing System.

handling characteristics of each storage mode. The economic analysis should recommend the appropriate picking mode for each item based on this matching of item requirements and storage mode capabilities. The Warehouse Toolbox™ automates this process. Table 6.3 below presents the productivity and cost characteristics of each case picking system alternative.

	Picking Rates (Cases/Hour)	Initial Cost
Pallet Jack	100 - 250	$1k to $10k/vehicle
Order Picker Truck	50 - 100	$30k/vehicle
Pick To Roller	125 - 250	$1k/ft.
Pick To Belt	250 - 400	$200/ft + $2k/divert
End-of-Aisle AS/RS	200 - 300	$300k to $450k/aisle

Table 6.3 Case Picking Systems Cost and Productivity Characteristics.

BROKEN CASE PICKING SYSTEMS

The major types of broken case picking systems are *picker-to-stock* (PTS) systems, *stock-to-picker* (STP) systems, and *automated dispensing*. In picker-to-stock systems the order picker walks or rides to the picking location. In stock-to-picker systems, the stock is mechanically (via carousel or AS/RS machine) transported to a stationary order picker. In automated item picking, items are automatically dispensed into shipping cartons or tote pans. In this section we will describe the pros, cons, applications, and associated costs of each of these major system types. As before, we will move through the system descriptions in order of increasing cost, complexity, and degree of automation.

PICKER-TO-STOCK SYSTEMS

In picker-to-stock systems, the order picker walks or rides to the picking location. The two sub-systems that must be selected are (1) the storage system that houses the stock and (2) the item retrieval system. The most popular alternatives for PTS storage systems and retrieval methods are reviewed below.

Picker-to-Stock Storage Systems

The three most popular picker-to-stock storage systems are bin shelving, modular storage drawers, and gravity flow rack.

Bin Shelving

Bin (or metal) shelving systems (Figure 6.26) are the oldest and still the most popular (in terms of sales volume and number of systems in use) equipment alternative for small parts order picking. Bin shelving systems are inexpensive ($100 to $150 per unit), easy to reconfigure and install, and require very little if any maintenance.

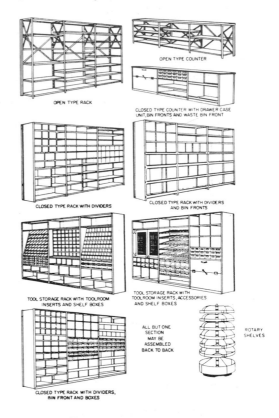

Figure 6.26 Bin Shelving.

Unfortunately, the lowest initial cost alternative may not be the most cost effective alternative, or the alternative which meets the prioritized needs of a warehouse. With bin shelving systems, savings in initial cost and maintenance may be offset by inflated space and labor requirements.

Since the full inside dimensions of a shelving unit are rarely usable, space is frequently underutilized in bin shelving systems. Also, since people may be walking and extracting the items, the height of bin shelving units is often limited to the reaching height of a human being. As a result, the available building cube is underutilized.

The consequences of low space utilization are twofold. First, low space utilization means that a large amount of floorspace is required to store the products. The more expensive it is to own and operate the space, the more expensive low space utilization becomes. Second, the greater the floorspace, the greater the area which must be traveled by the order pickers, and thus, the greater the labor requirement and costs.

Two additional drawbacks of bin shelving are supervisory problems and item security/protection problems. Supervisory problems arise because it is difficult to supervise people through a maze of bin shelving units. Security and item protection problems arise because bin shelving is open, i.e. all the items are exposed to and accessible from the picking aisles and by any operator and/or visitor.

Modular Storage Drawers in Cabinets

Modular storage drawers/cabinets (Figure 6.27) are called modular because each storage cabinet houses modular storage drawers which are subdivided into modular storage compartments. Drawer heights range from 3 inches to 24 inches, and each drawer may hold up to 400 pounds worth of material. Storage cabinets can be thought of as shelving units which house storage drawers.

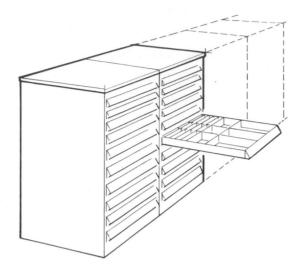

The primary advantage of storage drawers/cabinets over bin shelving is the large number of SKUs which can be stored and presented to the order picker in a small area. A single drawer can hold from 1 to 100 SKUs (depending on the size, shape, and inventory levels of the items), and a typical storage cabinet can store the equivalent of 2 to 4 shelving units worth of material. The excellent storage density accrues from the ability to create item housing configurations within a drawer/cabinet which very closely match the cubic storage requirements of each SKU. Also, since the drawers are pulled out into the aisle for picking, space does not have to be provided above each SKU to provide room for the order picker's hand and forearm. This reach space must be provided in bin shelving storage, otherwise items deep in the unit could not be accessed.

By housing more material in less floorspace, the overall space requirement for storage drawers is substantially less than that required for bin shelving. When the value of space is at a true premium, such as on a battle ship, on an airplane, on the manufacturing floor, or when facing the possibility of building additions, the reduction in space requirements alone can be enough to justify the use of storage drawers and cabinets.

Additional benefits achieved by the use of storage drawers include improved picking accuracy and protection for the items from the environment. Picking accuracy is improved over that in shelving units because the order picker's sight lines to the items are improved, and the quantity of light falling on the items to be extracted is increased. With bin shelving, the physical extraction of items may occur anywhere from floor level to 7 feet off the ground, with the order picker having to reach into the shelving unit itself to achieve the pick. With storage drawers, the drawer is pulled out into the picking aisle for item extraction. The order picker looks down onto the contents of the drawer which are illuminated by the light source for the picking aisle. (The fact that the order picker must look down on the drawer means that storage cabinets must be less than 5 feet in height.) Excellent item security and protection are achieved since the drawers can be closed and locked when not in use.

Storage cabinets equipped with drawers range in price from $1,000 to $1,500 per unit. Price is primarily a function of the number of drawers and the amount of sheet metal in the cabinet. Since the cost per cubic foot of storage is so high, storage drawers are only justifiable for items with very little on-hand cubic inventory (typically less than 0.5 cubic feet), and for operating scenarios in which the cost of space and the need for item security and protection are very high.

Gravity Flow Rack

Gravity flow rack (Figure 6.28) is typically used for SKUs with a high broken case cube movement and which are stored in fairly uniform sized and shaped cartons. Cartons are placed in the back of the rack from the replenishment aisle, and advance/roll towards the pick face as cartons are depleted from the front. The back-to-front movement insures first-in-first-out (FIFO) turnover of the material.

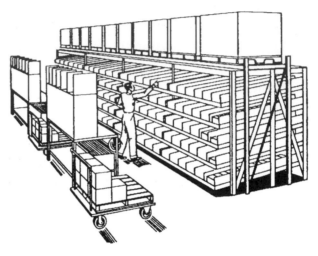

Figure 6.28 Gravity Flow Rack Picking Operation [25].

Essentially, a section of flow rack is a bin shelving unit turned perpendicular to the picking aisle with rollers placed on the shelves. The deeper the sections, the greater the portion of warehouse space that will be devoted to storage as opposed to aisle space. Further gains in space efficiency can be achieved by making use of the cubic space over the flow rack for full pallet storage.

Flow rack ranges in price from $3 to $10 per carton stored, depending on the length and weight capacity of the racks. As is the case with bin shelving, flow rack has very low

WORLD-CLASS WAREHOUSING © EDWARD H. FRAZELLE PH.D.

maintenance requirements and is available in a wide variety of standard section and lane sizes from a number of suppliers.

The fact that just one carton of each line item is located on the pick face means that a large number of SKUs are presented to the picker in a small area. Hence, walking and therefore labor requirements can be reduced with an efficient layout. (To make sure that the space behind the front carton is properly utilized, only the SKUs with two or more cartons on-hand should be assigned to positions in gravity flow rack.)

Space Saving Systems

Mezzanines and/or mobile storage systems can be employed to improve the utilization of building cube and floorspace in PTS systems.

Mezzanines

Bin shelving, modular storage cabinets, flow rack, and even carousels can be placed on a mezzanine (Figure 6.29). The advantage of using a mezzanine is that nearly twice as much material can be stored in the original floorspace. The major design issues for a mezzanine are the selection of the proper grade of mezzanine for the loading that will be experienced, the design of the material handling system to service the upper levels of the mezzanine, and the utilization of the available clear height. At least 14 feet of clear height should be available for a mezzanine to be considered. The cost of a typical mezzanine system is $10 to $20 per square foot.

The advantage of using a mezzanine is that nearly twice as much material can be stored in the original floorspace.

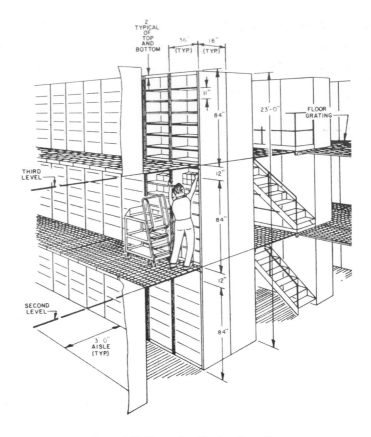

Figure 6.29 Mezzanine Picking Operation.

The key to maintaining high order picking productivity when a mezzanine is in use is to slot the products so that most of the picking activity takes place at the floor level. Consequently, the SKUs with the highest picking density should be assigned to the floor level and the SKUs with the lowest picking density should be assigned to the upper level. This ABC slotting policy with field picking of the upper level(s) yields excellent picking productivity. (Field picking is wave picking the upper level(s) prior to picking from the floor level. The contents of the wave are housed in designated bins on the floor level. Those bins are stops on the picking tours of the floor level.)

WORLD-CLASS WAREHOUSING © EDWARD H. FRAZELLE PH.D.

Mobile Storage Systems

Bin shelving, modular storage cabinets, and flow rack can all be "mobilized" (Figure 6.30). The most popular method of mobilization is the "train-track" method. Parallel tracks are cut into the floor, and wheels are placed on the bottom of the storage equipment to create "mobilized" equipment. The space savings accrue from the fact that only one aisle is needed between all the rows of storage equipment. The aisle is created by separating two adjacent rows of equipment. As a result, the aisle "floats" in the configuration between adjacent rows of equipment.

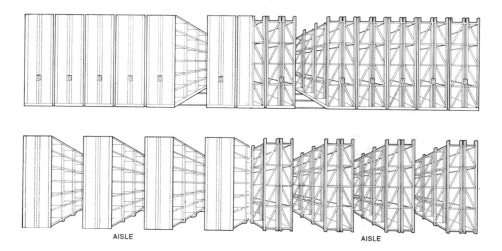

AISLE   AISLE

Figure 6.30 Mobile Bin Shelving System.

The storage equipment is moved by simply sliding the equipment along the tracks, by turning a crank located at the end of each storage row, or by invoking electric motors which provide the motive power. The disadvantage to this approach is the increased time required to access the items. Every time an item must be accessed, the corresponding storage aisle must be created. Hence, mobile storage systems should only be used for very slow moving items and when space is very scarce and/or expensive.

Picker-to-Stock Retrieval Systems

Picker-to-stock retrieval methods include cart picking, tote picking, man-aboard systems, and robotic item picking. The pros, cons, and applications of each are described below.

Cart Picking

A variety of picking carts (Figure 6.31) is available to facilitate accumulating, sorting, and/or packing orders as an order picker makes a picking tour. Batch picking carts are designed to allow an order picker to pick multiple orders on a picking tour, thus dramatically improving productivity as opposed to strict single order picking for small orders. Conventional carts provide dividers for order sortation, a place to hold paperwork and marking instruments, and a step ladder for picking at levels slightly above reaching height. More sophisticated carts automatically transport an order picker to a pick location, use light displays to direct the order picker to sort the contents of a pick into the correct order position, and permit mobile on-line communications via RF links and/or wireless local area network links. Cart picking rates range from 70 to 120 lines per person-hour.

Tote (or Carton) Picking

In tote picking systems (Figure 6.32), conveyors are used to transport tote pans (or shipping cartons) through successive picking zones to allow order completion. The tote pans are used to establish order integrity, for merchandise

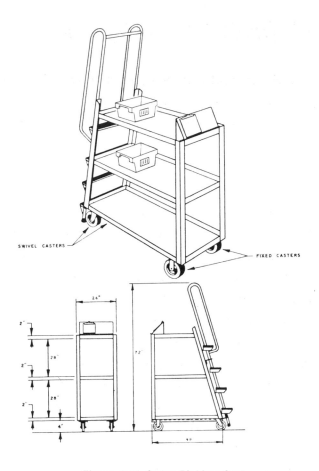

Figure 6.31 Order Picking Cart

accumulation and containment, and/or for shipping. Order pickers may walk one or more totes through a single picking zone, partially completing several orders at a time; or an order picker may walk one or more totes through all picking zones, thus completing one or more orders on each pass through the picking zones. Tote picking rates range from 150 to 300 lines per person-hour. The improvement over cart picking must be sufficient to justify the additional investment in conveying and sorting systems.

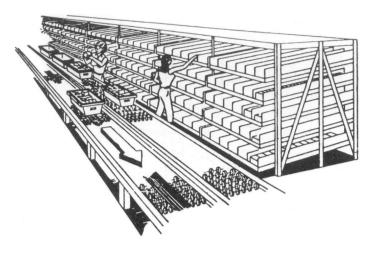

Figure 6.32 Tote Picking System (bottom illustration) [25].

Man-Up Systems

In the systems described thus far, the operator remains at floor level. To improve the utilization of building cube and floorspace, order pickers can ride up on an order picker truck or a man-aboard AS/RS machine to locations as high as 40 to 50 feet. The operation of order picker trucks was explained in section 6.2. The operation of a man-aboard AS/RS is described below.

A man-aboard AS/RS (Figure 6.33), as the name implies, is an automated storage and retrieval system in which the picker rides aboard a storage/retrieval machine to the pick locations. The storage locations may be provided by stacked bin shelving units, stacked storage cabinets, and/or pallet rack. The storage/ retrieval machine may be aisle captive or free roaming.

Typically, the order picker leaves from the front of the system at floor level and visits enough storage locations to fill one or multiple orders, depending on the order size. The

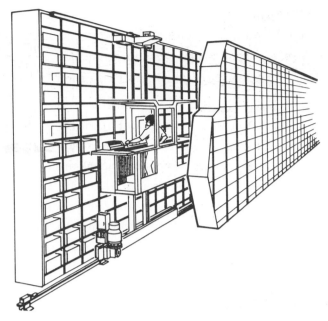

Figure 6.33 Man-Aboard AS/RS Picking Operation.

order picker can sort on-board if enough containers are provided on the storage/retrieval (S/R) machine.

A man-aboard AS/RS offers significant floorspace savings over the systems described so far. The floorspace savings are available because the storage system heights are no longer limited by the reach height of the order picker. Shelves or storage cabinets can be stacked as high as floor loading, weight capacity, throughput requirements, and/or ceiling heights will permit. The keys to achieving good picking productivity are intelligent slotting and pick tour sequencing. If there are ten or fewer picks per aisle traversal, then the objective is to keep most of the picks at or near floor level. If there are more than ten picks per aisle traversal, the operator should most likely be sequenced to make a sweep of the upper and lower levels of the aisle.

In that case, bands of fast moving items should be located in the upper and lower levels. The operator should traverse along the lower band on the way out from the i/o point and along the upper band on the way back to the i/o point.

Man-aboard automated storage and retrieval systems are far and away the most expensive picker-to-stock equipment alternative. Aisle-captive storage/retrieval machines reaching heights up to 40 feet cost around $125,000. Hence, there must be enough storage density and/or productivity improvement over cart and tote picking to justify the investment. Also, since vertical travel is slow compared to horizontal travel, typical picking rates in man-aboard operations range between 40 and 250 lines per person-hour. The range is large because there is a wide variety of operating schemes for man-aboard systems. Man-aboard systems are typically appropriate for slow moving items where space is fairly expensive.

Robotic Item Picking

Robotic picking vehicles (Figure 6.34) travel automatically through a sequence of picking locations receiving power and communication from rails in the floor and ceiling. The vehicles are equipped with a small carousel to permit order sortation, accumulation, and containment. The carousel travels up and down a mast on the robot as it traverses the picking aisle(s). The robot can automatically extract a storage drawer from a storage location onto the picking vehicle. The robot's arm is guided by an on-board vision system to direct item picking from a specific storage compartment in a storage drawer. Only in rare instances are robotic item picking systems justifiable.

Figure 6.34 Robotic Picking Vehicle.

STOCK-TO-PICKER SYSTEMS

The two major types of stock-to-picker systems are carousels and miniload automated storage/retrieval systems. Each system type is described below.

The major advantage of stock-to-picker systems over picker-to-stock systems is the elimination of the travel time for the order picker. When wage rates are high, the labor savings can be sufficient to justify the investment in the mechanical and control systems required in STP systems. If a STP system is not designed properly, an order picker may remain idle waiting on the system to present the next picking transaction. In those cases, productivity can actually be worse than that found in PTS systems.

Another advantage of STP systems is supervision. In STP systems, the picking takes place at the end of an aisle. Hence, all of the operators should be visible to a supervisor in one quick glance down a picking line.

Carousels

Carousels, as the name implies, are mechanical devices which house and rotate items for order picking. Horizontal and vertical carousels are popular for order picking applications.

Horizontal Carousels

A horizontal carousel (Figure 6.35) is a linked series of rotating bins of adjustable shelves driven on the top or on the bottom by a drive motor unit. Rotation takes place about an axis perpendicular to the floor at a rate of about 80 to 120 feet per minute.

Items are extracted from the carousel by order pickers who occupy fixed positions in front of the carousel(s). Order pickers may also be responsible for controlling the rotation of the carousel. Manual control is achieved via a keypad which tells the carousel which bin location to rotate forward and a foot pedal, which releases the carousel to rotate. Carousels may also be computer controlled, in which case the sequence of pick locations is stored in a computer and brought forward automatically.

The assignment of order pickers to carousels is flexible. If an order picker is assigned to one carousel unit, he or she

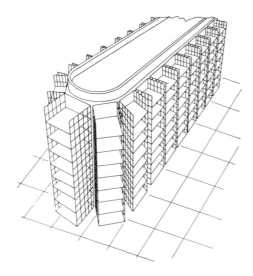

Figure 6.35 Horizontal Carousel System.

must wait for the carousel to rotate to the correct location between picks. If an order picker is assigned to two or more carousels, he or she may pick from one carousel while the other is rotating to the next pick location. Remember, the objective of stock-to-picker systems is to keep the picker picking. (Humans are excellent extractors of items; the flexibility of our limbs and muscles provides us with this capability. We are not efficient searchers, walkers, or waiters.)

Horizontal carousels vary in length from 15 feet to 100 feet, and in height from 6 feet to 25 feet. The length and height of the units are dictated by the pick rate requirements and building restrictions. The longer the carousel, the more time required, on average, to rotate the carousel to the desired location. Also, the taller the carousel, the more time required to access the items. Heights over 6 feet require the use of ladders, lift platforms, or robot arms on vertical masts to access the items.

One drawback of horizontal carousels is that the throughput capacity is limited by the rotation speed of the motor drive. Another drawback is the initial investment of $40,000 to $70,000 per carousel unit. Consequently, items with a high cube movement should not be housed in carousels since the carousel may not be able to rotate fast enough to permit sufficient access to those items and since those items would occupy a large and expensive envelope of space in the carousel.

A double-face horizontal carousel (Figure 6.36) was recently introduced to the material handling market. In the double-face carousel, the traditional carousel carrier is split vertically in half and rotated 90 degrees. This design allows for more, shallower pick faces; thus improving the storage density for small parts. In addition, this design hides the pick face for all the items except those presented to the order picker, thus improving item protection and security.

Figure 6.36 Double-Face Horizontal Carousel [White].

WORLD-CLASS WAREHOUSING © EDWARD H. FRAZELLE PH.D.

Vertical Carousels

A vertical carousel (Figure 6.37) is a horizontal carousel turned on its end and enclosed in sheet metal. As with horizontal carousels, an order picker operates one or multiple carousels. The carousels are indexed either automatically via computer control, or manually by the order picker working a keypad on the carousel's work surface.

Vertical carousels range in height from 8 feet to 35 feet. Heights (as lengths were for horizontal carousels) are dictated by throughput requirements and building restrictions. The taller the system, the longer it will take, on average, to rotate the desired bin location to the pick station.

Order pick times for vertical carousels are theoretically less than those for horizontal carousels. The decrease results from the fact that items are always presented at an order picker's waist level. This eliminates the stooping and reaching that goes on with horizontal carousels, further reduces search time, and promotes more accurate picking. (Some of the gains in item extract time are negated by the slower rotation speed of the vertical carousel. Recall that the direction of rotation is against gravity.)

Additional benefits provided by the vertical carousel include excellent item protection and security. In the vertical carousel, only one shelf of items is exposed at one time, and the entire contents of the carousel can be locked up.

The cost of a typical vertical carousel is around $100,000, increasing with the number of shelves, weight capacity, and special features and controls. The additional cost of vertical carousels over horizontal carousels is a result of the sheet metal enclosure, and the extra power required to rotate against the force of gravity.

Figure 6.37 Vertical Carousel [Remstar].

Miniload Automated Storage and Retrieval Systems

In miniload automated storage and retrieval systems (Figure 6.38), an automated storage/retrieval (S/R) machine travels horizontally and vertically simultaneously in a storage aisle, transporting storage containers to and from an order picking station located at one end of the system. The order picking station typically has two pick positions. As the order picker is picking from the container in the left pick position, the S/R machine is taking the container from the right pick position back to its location in the rack and returning with the next container. The result is that an order picker alternately picks from the left and right pick positions.

The sequence of containers to be processed can be determined manually (the order picker keying in the desired line item numbers or rack locations on a keypad) or automatically by computer control.

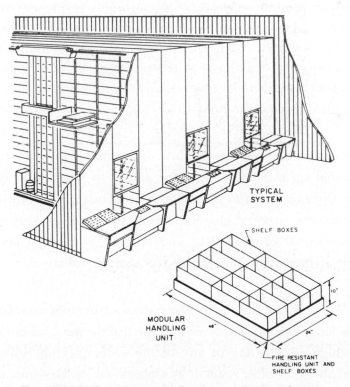

Figure 6.38 Miniload Automated Storage and Retrieval System.

Miniloads vary in height from 8 to 50 feet, and in length from 40 to 200 feet. As in the case with carousels, the height and length of the system are dictated by the throughput requirements and building restrictions. The longer and taller the system, the longer the time required to access the containers. However, the longer and taller the system, the fewer the aisles and S/R machines that will have to be purchased. At between $150,000 and $300,000 per aisle, the determination of the correct system length, height, and number of aisles to meet the pick rate, storage, and economic return requirements for the warehouse is critical.

The transaction rate capacity of the miniload is governed by the ability of the S/R machine (which travels approximately 500 feet per minute horizontally and 120 feet per minute vertically) to continuously present the order picker with unprocessed storage containers. This ability, coupled with the human factors benefits of presenting the containers to the picker at waist height in a well lit area, can yield pick rates ranging between 40 and 200 picks per person-hour.

Floorspace requirements are low due to the ability to store material up to 50 feet high, the ability to size and shape the storage containers and the subdivisions of those containers to very closely match the storage volume requirements of each SKU, and an aisle width that need only accommodate the width of a storage container.

The new systems can be installed in a few months and are less expensive and more reliable than their predecessors.

As the most sophisticated of the system alternatives described thus far, it should come as no surprise that the miniload carries the highest price tag of any of the order picking system alternatives. Another result of its sophistication is the significant engineering and design time that accompanies each system.

WORLD-CLASS WAREHOUSING © EDWARD H. FRAZELLE PH.D.

Most systems require between 6 and 24 months for design, delivery and installation. Finally, greater sophistication leads to greater maintenance requirements. It is only through a disciplined maintenance program that miniload suppliers are able to advertise up-time percentages between 97% and 99.5%.

Fortunately, a group of new miniload suppliers are making pre-engineered, modular systems. The new systems can be installed in a few months and are less expensive and more reliable than their predecessors.

Automated Dispensing

Automated item dispensing systems (Figure 6.39) act much like vending machines for small items of uniform

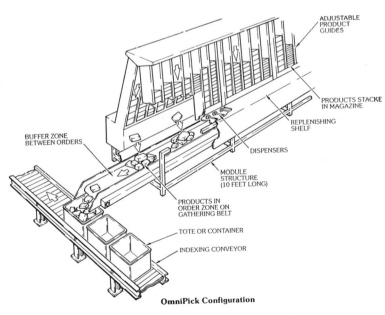

OmniPick Configuration

Figure 6.39a Automated Dispensing Machine [Electrocom].

size and shape. Each item is allocated a vertical dispenser ranging from 2 to 6 inches wide and from 3 to 5 feet tall. (The width of each dispenser is easily adjusted to accommodate variable product sizes.) The dispensing mechanism acts to kick the unit of product at the bottom of the dispenser out onto a conveyor running between two rows of dispensers configured as an A-Frame over a belt conveyor. A tiny vacuum conveyor or small finger on a chain conveyor is used to dispense the items.

Figure 6.39b Automated Order Picking Operation [SI Handling].

Virtual order windows begin at one end of the conveyor and pass by each dispenser. If an item is required in the order window, it is dispensed onto the conveyor. Merchandise is accumulated at the end of the belt conveyor into a tote pan or carton. A single dispenser can dispense at a rate of up to 6 units per second. Automatic item pickers are popular in industries with high throughput for small items of uniform size and shape, such as cosmetics, wholesale drugs, compact discs, videos, publications, and polybagged garments.

Replenishment is performed manually from the back of the system. The manual replenishment operation significantly cuts into the potential savings in picking labor requirements. Nonetheless, typical picking rates are in the range of 1,500 to 2,000 picks per person-hour. Typical picking accuracy is 99.97%.

One new design for automated dispensing machines is an inverted A-Frame (Figure 6.40) which streamlines the replenishment of automated dispensers and increases the storage density along the picking line. In so doing, the price per dispenser has been reduced from nearly $650 per dispenser, to around $250. Another new design allows automated dispensing for polybagged garments.

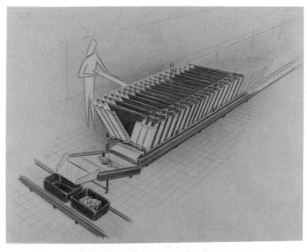

Figure 6.40 Inverted A-Frame Automated Dispensing Machine [Electrocom].

Broken Case Picking Systems Comparison and Selection

As is the case in all of the systems selections and justifications described so far, a picking mode economic analysis should be conducted to assign each item to its most economically attractive storage mode. This analysis should consider the activity and inventory profile of each item and the storage and handling characteristics of each storage mode. The economic analysis should recommend the appropriate storage mode for each item based on this matching of item requirements and storage mode capabilities. The *Warehouse Toolbox* automates this process. Table 6.4 below presents the summary characteristics of each broken case picking system.

Figure 6.41 illustrates an example broken case picking mode economic analysis. The figure shows the optimal assignment of items to picking modes based on each item's cube movement and picking density.

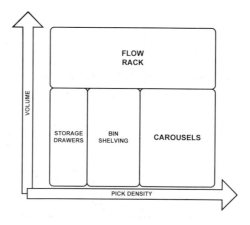

Figure 6.41 Example Broken Case Picking Mode Economic Analysis [Warehouse Toolbox].

System Attribute	Unit of Measure	Bin Shelving	Gravity Flow Racks	Storage Drawers	Horizontal Carousel	Vertical Carousel	Miniload ASRS	Automatic Dispensing
Gross System Cost	Initial Cost/ Purchased Ft3	$5-$15	$3-$5	$25-$30	$20-$35	$40-$70	$30-$40	$300-$600 per dispenser
Net System Cost	Initial Cost/ Available Ft3.	$10-$30	$9-$15	$31-$38	$40-$70	$65-$100	$38-$50	
Floorspace Requirements	Ft3 of inventory housed per Ft2 of Floorspace.	1-1.2	0.7-0.85	1.8-2.5	0.8-1.25	5.0-6.0	4.0-5.0	
Human Factors	Ease of retrieval.	Average	Average	Good	Average	Excellent	Excellent	Good
Maintenance Requirements		Low	Low	Low	Medium	Medium	High	High
Item Security		Average	Average	Excellent	Good	Excellent	Excellent	Average
Flexibility	Ease to Reconfigure	High	High	High	Medium	Low	Low	Low
Pick Rate	Order Lines per Person-Hour	C: 25-125 T: 100-350 M: 25-250 W: 300-500	C: 25-125 T: 100-350 M: 25-250 W: 300-500	C: 25-125 T: 100-350 M: 25-250 W: 300-500	50-250	50-300	25-125	500-1000
Key	T = Tote Picking	C = Cart Picking	M = Man Aboard ASRS	W = Wave Picking				

Table 6.4 Summary Characteristics of Alternative Broken Case Picking Systems.

6.4
SUMMARY

Intelligent application of mechanized systems for pallet, case, and item handling can yield significant improvements in all of the warehouse key performance indicators including productivity, accuracy, response time, and storage density. Using incremental justification, mechanized systems can also contribute positively to the financial performance of a warehouse. In either case, the designers' and decision makers' awareness and understanding of system features and costs determines the ultimate satisfaction with a mechanized system. Toward that end, this chapter presents the pros, cons, costs, and applications of the major systems used in pallet storage and retrieval, case picking, and loose item picking.

WORLD-CLASS WAREHOUSING © EDWARD H. FRAZELLE PH.D.

WAREHOUSE LAYOUT

The process of laying out a warehouse is a lot like putting a puzzle together. And like a puzzle, it is difficult to complete until all the pieces have been defined and assembled. Defining those pieces is the purpose of profiling, benchmarking, simplifying, computerizing, and mechanizing warehouse operations. In these five steps, we work to define individual processes and the types of material handling and storage systems working inside the warehouse. Putting those processes and systems together in a synergistic and flexible floorspace and building layout is the subject of this chapter.

A five-step methodology for warehouse layout is presented below. The methodology requires as input the warehouse activity profile, the performance goals for the operation, the definition and configuration of the warehouse processes, and the configuration of all material handling and storage systems.

SPACE REQUIREMENTS PLANNING

A warehouse layout should be based on the space requirements for and the interrelationships between individual warehouse processes. The first step in laying out a warehouse is to determine the overall space requirements for all warehouse processes. The space requirements for each process should be computed and summarized to estimate the overall building requirements. An example format for recording and summarizing the space requirements for a warehouse is provided in Table 7.1.

Process	Floorspace Requirements (Square Feet)	Notes and Comments
1. Receiving Staging	30,000	
2. Pallet Storage	120,000	
3. Case Picking	25,000	
4. Broken Case Picking	15,000	
5. Packing & Unitizing	15,000	
6. Customizing	20,000	
7. Accumulation & Sorting	30,000	
8. Shipping Staging	30,000	
9. Cross-Docking	15,000	
10. Warehouse Offices	15,000	
11. Restrooms	5,000	
Sub-total	320,000	
Inter-activity Aisle Allowance	64,000	@ 20% of Sub-total
TOTAL	384,000	

Table 7.1 Warehouse Space Requirements Worksheet.

Receiving and shipping staging space is a function of the number of receiving and shipping dock doors and the turnaround time for each dock. A common practice is to allocate enough staging space behind each dock door to accommodate a truckload's worth of material.

Floorspace requirements for pallet storage and retrieval, case picking, and broken case picking should be computed as part of the picking mode economic analysis and in slotting (see section 4.5).

Floorspace requirements for packing and unitizing, customizing, and/or accumulation and sortation are computed as a function of the floorspace required for each work station in those areas, the number of work stations required, and the material handling methods employed in each area.

Warehouse office space is simply a function of the number of offices and the floorspace required for each. The floorspace required for restrooms can be computed from local building code requirements.

The sum of the floorspace requirements for each process is a sub-total to which an inter-process aisle allowance is added to yield total floorspace requirements. More detailed descriptions of warehouse sizing and floorspace estimation procedures are included in [21, 23]. The following case example illustrates a high-level warehouse sizing and floorspace requirements estimation exercise.

A warehouse layout should be based on the space requirements for and the interrelationships between individual warehouse processes.

Heavy Machinery Inc. (HMI)

We were asked on a recent project to project the aggregate warehousing space requirements for HMI for the next five years. Since pallet storage is the most space intensive process in a warehouse, we began by computing the storage space requirements for pallets. The computations are described below and summarized in Table 7.2 (In this simple analysis I used data gathered in the warehouse activity profile to project the floorspace requirement for pallet storage.)

i.) Divide forecasted unit sales (from marketing projections) by annual inventory turns (from material management) to compute the average unit inventory.

ii.) Divide the average unit inventory by the average units per pallet (from the item master file) to compute the average pallet inventory.

iii.) Multiply the average pallet inventory by the ratio of peak-to-average (PTA) inventory (from the item master file) to compute the peak pallet inventory.

iv.) Multiply the peak pallet inventory by the portion of peak inventory used for storage planning purposes to compute the effective pallet storage capacity.

v.) Divide the effective pallet storage capacity by the location utilization factor (typically 85% for single-deep pallet storage) to compute the required number of pallet storage locations.

vi.) Divide the required number of pallet storage locations by the storage density (square feet per pallet computed as a function of the aisle width and storage height) to compute the floorspace requirements.

Year	Forecasted Unit Sales	Turns	Average Inventory	Average Pallets	PTA	% Peak	Util.	Storage Locations Required	Aisles	Levels	Density	Space
1993	381,244	12	31,770	626	1.08	0.93	0.85	740	9	3	12	8,882
1994	406,478	12	33,873	668	1.08	0.93	0.85	789	9	3	12	9,470
1995	423,600	12	35,300	696	1.08	0.93	0.85	822	9	3	12	9,869
1996	449,000	12	37,417	738	1.08	0.93	0.85	872	9	3	12	10,461
1997	475,000	12	39,583	780	1.08	0.93	0.85	922	9	3	12	11,066
1998	504,900	12	42,075	830	1.08	0.93	0.85	980	9	3	12	11,763

Table 7.2. Example Pallet Floorspace Requirements Computations [The Progress Group].

Floorspace requirements in a given area and in the overall layout can and should be reduced by:

· running storage lanes and racking parallel to the long axis of the building,

· implementing a random storage location policy in large storage areas,

· utilizing over-aisle (Figure 7.1) and over-dock storage when feasible,

· burying building columns in storage racks, and

· running storage lanes and racking along interior walls.

Specify a U-shape, straight-thru, or modular overall flow design.

7.2
MATERIAL FLOW PLANNING

In flow planning we specify a U-shape, straight-thru, or modular overall flow plan. An example U-shape warehouse flow design is illustrated in Figure 7.2. In the classic case,

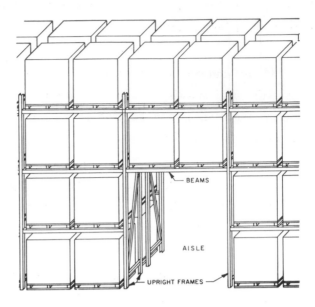

Figure 7.1 Over-Aisle Storage.

products flow in at receiving, move into storage in the back of the warehouse, and then to shipping which is located adjacent to receiving on the same side of the building.

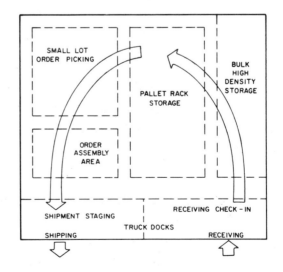

Figure 7.2 Typical U-shaped Flow Pattern.

A U-shape flow design has a number of advantages over other flow designs including:

·   excellent utilization of dock resources (dock doors, dock equipment, dock space, dock operators, and dock supervisors) since the receiving and shipping processes can share dock doors;

·   facilitating cross-docking since the receiving and shipping docks are adjacent to one another and may be co-mingled; and

·   excellent lift truck utilization since putaway and retrieval trips are easily combined and since the storage locations closest to the receiving and shipping docks are natural locations to house fast moving items.

With these inherent advantages, the U-shape flow design is the benchmark upon which all other flow designs should be compared.

An example straight-thru flow design is illustrated in Figure 7.3. The straight-thru configuration lends itself to operations that are pure cross-docking facilities (sometimes referred to as flow-through facilities) or operations in which the peak receiving and shipping times coincide.

An example modular flow design is illustrated in Figures 7.4. Modular flow design is well suited for large-scale operations in which individual processes are so large they merit stand-alone and uniquely designed buildings. Examples include rack-supported buildings for a unit load AS/RS; an air con

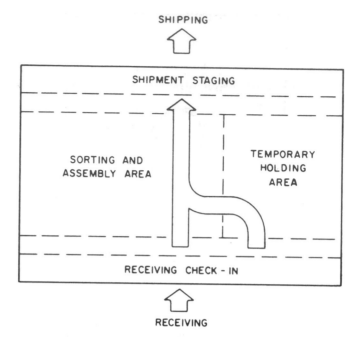

SHIPPING

SHIPMENT STAGING

SORTING AND
ASSEMBLY AREA

TEMPORARY
HOLDING
AREA

RECEIVING CHECK - IN

RECEIVING

Figure 7.3a Typical Straight-Thru Flow Design.

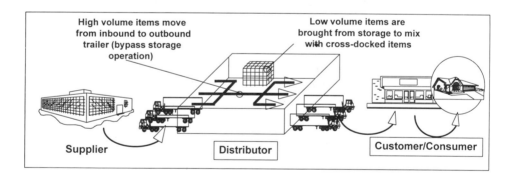

High volume items move
from inbound to outbound
trailer (bypass storage
operation)

Low volume items are
brought from storage to mix
with cross-docked items

Supplier

Distributor

Customer/Consumer

Figure 7.3b Example Straight-Thru Flow Design for a Grocery
Flow-Thru Operation [24].

ditioned low bay building for customizing operations such
as monogramming, pricing and marking; or a low-bay shipping building equipped with high-speed sortation equipment.

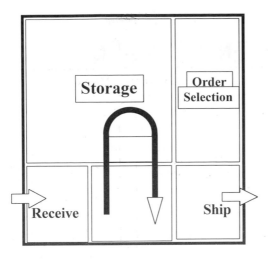

Figure 7.4a Example Modular Flow Design.

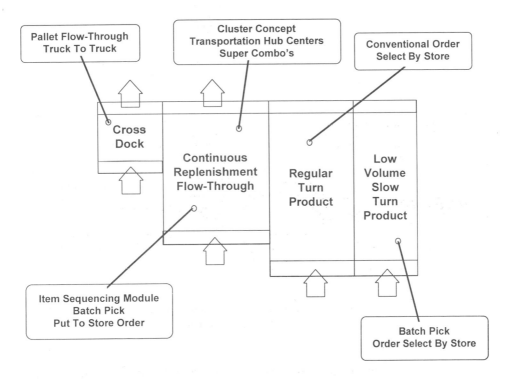

Figure 7.4b Example modular flow design with modules designed
specifically for cross-docking (low-bay), continuous replenishment
(medium bay), and medium and slow-moving items (high-bay) [24].

7.3
ADJACENCY PLANNING

Based primarily on material flow patterns, processes with high adjacency requirements should be located close to one another. For example, reserve storage should be located near receiving since there is typically a lot of material flow between receiving and reserve storage. The same can be said for receiving and cross-docking, cross-docking and shipping, case picking and pallet storage, case picking and broken case picking, picking activities and customizing and unitizing activities, and customizing and unitizing activities with shipping. These natural flow relationships often lead to the U-shape flow design illustrated in Figure 7.2.

A warehouse activity relationship chart is used to document the adjacency requirements of the processes in a warehouse. Figure 7.5 gives examples of warehouse activity relationship charts. Computer-aided facility layout tools such as CRAFT, CORELAP, and ALDEP [21] take these adjacency requirements, the floorspace requirements of each process, and the location of fixed objects as inputs and compute an optimal block layout for a facility. These tools are initiated with the location of fixed elements including columns, exit doors, dock doors, railroad tracks, highways, etc. so that processes may be oriented toward or away from them as necessary.

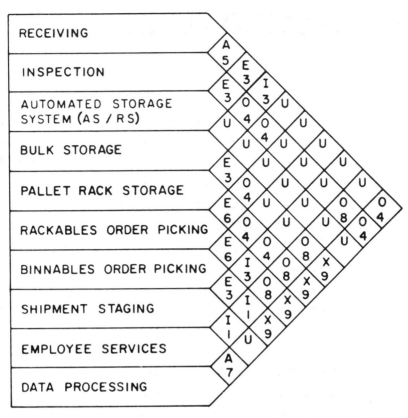

RECEIVING

INSPECTION

AUTOMATED STORAGE SYSTEM (AS / RS)

BULK STORAGE

PALLET RACK STORAGE

RACKABLES ORDER PICKING

BINNABLES ORDER PICKING

SHIPMENT STAGING

EMPLOYEE SERVICES

DATA PROCESSING

REASONS FOR IMPORTANCE

1. Supervision
2. Safety
3. Material flow
4. Work flow
5. Material control
6. Equipment proximity
7. Shared spaced
8. Employee Health and Safety
9. Security

PROXIMITY IMPORTANCE

A. Absolutely necessary
E. Especially important
I. Important
O. Ordinary closeness
U. Unimportant
X. Undesirable

Figure 7.5a Example Warehouse Activity Relationship Chart [25].

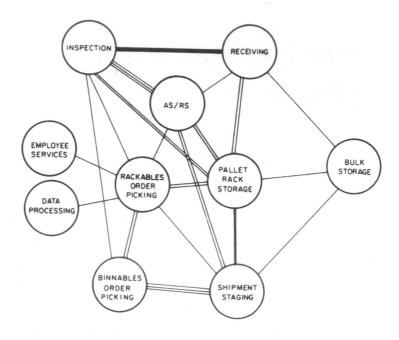

Figure 7.5b Activity Relationship Diagram (heavy lines
indicate high adjacency requirements) [25].

PROCESS LOCATION

*Assign processes
with high storage re-
quirements to high-
bay space, and labor
intensive processes
in low bay space.*

One of the major reasons for low space utilization in warehouse facilities is that processes that can be executed in low-
bay space - receiving, broken case picking, customization,
returns processing, etc. - are often executed in high-bay space.
If the high-bay space is existing, it can be mezzanined to
accommodate multiple low-bay processes in the same
floorspace. The key design principle is to assign processes
with high storage requirements to high-bay space, and labor intensive processes to low-bay space.

7.5
EXPANSION/CONTRACTION PLANNING

The only thing we know about tomorrow is that it will be different from today. In a warehouse, different may mean larger or smaller, faster or slower, more variety or less variety, taller or shorter, more people or fewer people, more technology or less technology, etc. To accommodate the rapid pace of change, a carefully configured warehouse layout includes expansion and contraction plans for each area in the warehouse and for the warehouse as a whole. An example warehouse expansion plan is illustrated in Figure 7.6.

Document expansion and contraction strategies for each warehouse process.

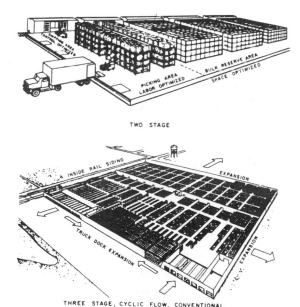

TWO STAGE

THREE STAGE, CYCLIC FLOW, CONVENTIONAL

Figure 7.6a Warehouse Expansion Concept [25].

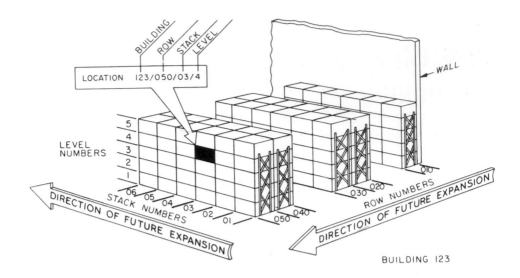

Figure 7.6b Rack Expansion Plan [25].

7.6
SUMMARY

Use principles 1-5 as a checklist to insure that your warehouse layout meets world-class standards.

1.   Determine the overall space requirements for all warehouse processes.

2.   Specify a U-shape, straight-thru, or modular overall flow design.

3.   Locate functions with high adjacency requirements close to one another.

4.   Assign processes with high storage requirements to high-bay space, and labor intensive processes in low-bay space.

5.   Document expansion and contraction strategies for each warehouse process.

REFERENCES

1. Gagnon, E., *Managing People in the Warehouse*, MARGO, Minnetonka, Minnesota, 1993.

2. Camp, Robert C., *Benchmarking*, Quality Press, Milwaukee, 1989.

3. International Benchmarking Clearinghouse, American Productivity and Quality Center, Houston, Texas.

4. *Modern Materials Handling*, Cahners Publishing, Newton, Massachusetts.

5. *Warehouse Productivity Analysis Report*, National-American Wholesale Grocers Association, Wasldorf, Maryland, 1995.

6. "1995 Benchmarking Survey," The Logistics Institute, Georgia Institute of Technology, Atlanta, Georgia, 1995.

7. Davis, Herbert, "Distribution Costs and Customer Service Levels: How Do You Compare in 1989?" *Proceedings of the 1989 Council of Logistics*

Management Annual Conference, Council of Logistics Management, Oak Brook, IL, 1992.

8. Frazelle, E.H. and S.T. Hackman, "The Warehouse Performance Index: A Single-Point Metric for Benchmarking Warehouse Performance," Material Handling Research Center, Georgia Institute of Technology, 1993.

9. *Warehouse Toolbox*, Logistics Technology Group, Nashville, Tennessee.

10. Waterson, Karen, *Client/Server Technology for Managers*, Addison-Wesley, Reading, Massachusetts, 1995.

11. Taylor, David A., *Business Engineering with Object Technology*, Wiley, New York, 1995.

12. *Logistics Software Overview*, Andersen Consulting, Atlanta, Georgia,1994.

13. "A Guide for Evaluating and Implementing a Warehouse Bar Code System," Warehousing Education and Research Council, Oak Brook, Illinois, 1992.

14. Automatic Identification Systems for Material Handling and MaterialManagement, Automatic Identification Manufacturers Product Section, Materials Handling Institute, Charlotte, NC, 1976.

15. Hill, J.M., "Automatic Identification from A to Z," *Proceedings of the 1993 Material Handling Short Course*, Georgia Institute of Technology, Atlanta, Georgia, 1993.

16. Apple, J. M., *Material Handling Systems Design*, Ronald Press, New York, 1972.

17. Frazelle, E. H., *Material Handling Systems and Terminology*, Lionhart Publishing, Atlanta, Georgia, 1992.

18. Frazelle, E. H. and J.M. Apple, Jr., "Material Handling Technologies," *The Logistics Handbook* (W. A. Copacino, Editor), Macmillan, New York, 1993.

19. Kulwiec, R., "Material Handling Equipment Guide," *Plant Engineering*, August 21, 1980, pp. 88-99.

20. *Materials Handling Handbook* (Raymond A. Kulwiec, Editor), John Wiley & Sons, New York, 1985.

21. Tompkins, J.A., J.A. White, Y.A. Bozer, E.H. Frazelle, J. Tanchoco, J. Trevino, *Facilities Planning*, John Wiley, New York, 1996.

22. Material Handling Institute, Charlotte, North Carolina.

23. Kinney, H. D., "How to Size the Warehouse, *Material Handling Management Course*, American Institute of Industrial Engineers, Norcross, Ga., June 1979.

24. Strahan, Bruce A., "The Logistics of Supply Chain Integration," *Proceedings of the Logistics Short Course*, The Logistics Institute, Georgia Institute of Technology, April, 1995.

25. *Warehouse Modernization and Layout Planning Guide*, U.S. Naval Supply Systems Command Publication 529, U.S. Naval Supply Systems Command, Richmond, Virginia, 1988.

BIBLIOGRAPHY

"A Guide for Evaluating and Implementing a Warehouse Bar Code System," Warehousing Education and Research Council, Oak Brook, Illinois, 1992.

Apple, J. M., *Material Handling Systems Design*, Ronald Press, New York, 1972.

Apple, J. M., *Plant Layout and Material Handling*, Ronald Press, 3rd ed., New York, 1977.

Apple, J. M. Jr. and B.A. Strahan, "Proper Planning and Control-The Keys to Effective Storage," *Industrial Engineering*, vol. 13, no. 4, pp. 102-112, April 1981.

Automatic Identification Systems for Material Handling and Material Management, Automatic Identification Manufacturers Product Section, Materials Handling Institute, Charlotte, NC, 1976.

Camp, Robert C., *Benchmarking*, Quality Press, Milwaukee, 1989.

Considerations for Planning and Installing an Automated Storage/Retrieval System, Automated Storage/Retrieval

Systems Product Section, Material Handling Institute, Charlotte, NC, 1977.

Davis, Herbert, "Distribution Costs and Customer Service Levels: How Do You Compare in 1989?" *Proceedings of the 1989 Council of Logistics Management Annual Conference*, Council of Logistics Management, Oak Brook, IL, 1989.

Drury, J., "Towards More Efficient Order Picking," IMM Monograph Number 1, The Institute of Materials Management, Cranfield, United Kingdom (1988).

Frazelle, E.H., *Material Handling Systems and Terminology*, Lionhart Publishing, Atlanta, Georgia, 1992.

Frazelle, E.H., "Stock Location Assignment and Order Picking Productivity," Doctoral Dissertation, Georgia Institute of Technology, Atlanta, Georgia, 1989.

Frazelle, E.H., *Warehouse Audit Workbook*, Logistics Resources International, Atlanta, Georgia, 1995.

Frazelle, E. H. and J.M. Apple, Jr., "Material Handling Technologies," *The Logistics Handbook* (W. A. Copacino, Editor), Macmillan, New York, 1993.

Frazelle, E. H. and J.M. Apple, Jr., "Warehouse Operations," *The Distribution Management Handbook* (J.A. Tompkins, Editor), McGraw-Hill, New York, 1993.

Frazelle, E. H. and L.F. McGinnis, "Automated Material Handling" in *The Encyclopedia of Microcomputers* (A. Kent and J.G. Williams, Editors), Marcel- Dekker, New York and Basel, 1988.

Frazelle, E. H. and R.E. Ward, "Material Handling Technologies in Japan," National Technical Information Service Report #PB93-128197, Washington, D.C., 1992.

Frazelle, E.H. and S.T. Hackman, "The Warehouse Performance Index: A Single-Point Metric for Benchmarking Warehouse Performance," Material Handling Research Center, Georgia Institute of Technology, 1993.

Frazelle, E. H., S.T. Hackman, and L.K. Platzman, "Intelligent Stock Assignment Planning, *Proceeding of the 1989 Council of Logistics Management's Annual Conference*, St. Louis, MO., October 1989.

Frazelle, E. H., S.T. Hackman, and L.K. Platzman, "Intelligent Stock Assignment Planning, *Proceeding of the 1989 Council of Logistics Management's Annual Conference*, St. Louis, MO., October 1989.

Frazelle, E. H., S.T. Hackman, U. Passy, and L.K. Platzman, "The Forward-Reserve Problem, *Optimization in Industry*, Wiley, New York, 1994.

Gagnon, E., *Managing People in the Warehouse*, MARGO, Minnetonka, Minnesota, 1993.

Goetschalckx, M. and H.D. Ratliff, "Sequencing Picking Operations in a Man-Aboard Order Picking System," *Material Flow*, Vol. 4, No. 4, 1988, pp. 255-263.

Graves, S.C., W.H. Hausman, and L.B. Schwarz, "Storage Retrieval Interleaving in Automatic Warehousing Systems," *Management Science*, Vol. 23, No. 9 (May 1977), pp. 935-945.

Hill, J.M., "Automatic Identification Perspective 1992, *Proceedings of the Material Handling Short Course*, Georgia Institute of Technology, Atlanta, Georgia, March 1992.

Hill, J.M., "Automatic Identification from A to Z," *Proceedings of the 1993 Material Handling Short Course*, Georgia Institute of Technology, Atlanta, Georgia, 1993.

Hill, J.M., "Warehouse Management Systems Perspective 1994," Cypress Associates, Monterrey, California, 1994.

International Benchmarking Clearinghouse, American Productivity and Quality Center, Houston, Texas.

Kinney, H. D., "How to Size the Warehouse, *Material Handling Management Course*, American Institute of Industrial Engineers, Norcross, Ga., June 1979.

Kulwiec, R., "Material Handling Equipment Guide," *Plant Engineering*, August 21, 1980, pp. 88-99.

"Lift Truck Attachments," *Modern Materials Handling*, vol. 32, no. 8, pp. 55-64, August 1977.

Logistics Software Overview, Andersen Consulting, Atlanta, Georgia, 1994.

Material Handling Engineering, Penton Publishing, Cleveland, Ohio.

Materials Handling Handbook (Raymond A. Kulwiec, Editor), John Wiley & Sons, New York, 1985.

Material Handling Institute, Charlotte, North Carolina.

Measuring and Improving Productivity in Physical Distribution, Council of Logistics Management, Oak Brook, IL, 1984.

Modern Materials Handling, Cahners Publishing, Newton, Massachusetts.

"Radio Frequency Data Communications," Warehousing Education and Research Council, Oak Brook, Illinois, 1993.

Strahan, Bruce A., "The Logistics of Supply Chain Integration," *Proceedings of the Logistics Short Course*, The Logistics Institute, Georgia Institute of Technology, April, 1995.

Suzuki, J., "Guide to the Installation of Automated Sorters," *1990 International Conference on Automation in Warehousing Proceedings*, Institute of Industrial Engineers, Atlanta, Georgia.

Taylor, David A., *Business Engineering with Object Technology*, Wiley, New York, 1995.

The Progress Group., *"Logistics Master Planning"*, Atlanta, Georgia. 1995.

Tompkins, J.A., J.A. White, Y.A. Bozer, E.H. Frazelle, J. Tanchoco, J. Trevino, *Facilities Planning*, John Wiley, New York, 1996.

Warehousing Management, Chilton Publishing, Radnor, Pennsylvania.

Warehouse Modernization and Layout Planning Guide, U.S. Naval Supply Systems Command Publication 529, U.S. Naval Supply Systems Command, Richmond, Virginia, 1988.

Warehouse Toolbox, Logistics Technology Group, Nashville, Tennessee.

Warehouse Productivity Analysis Report, National-American Wholesale Grocers Association, Wasldorf, Maryland, 1995.

Waterson, Karen, *Client/Server Technology for Managers*, Addison-Wesley, Reading, Massachusetts, 1995.

White, J.A., *Yale Management Guide to Productivity*, Yale Industrial Truck Division, Eaton Corp., Philadelphia, Pa., 1978.

Zollinger, H.A., "Do It Yourself Guide to Costing Stacker Systems," *Automation*, vol. 21, pp. 90-93, September 1974.

Zollinger, H.A., "Planning, Evaluating, and Estimating Storage Systems," Presented at Institute of Material

Management Education First Annual Winter Seminar Series, Orlando, Florida, February 1982.

"1995 Benchmarking Survey," The Logistics Institute, Georgia Institute of Technology, Atlanta, Georgia, 1995.